FUN WITH MATHS

392 Mathematical Enchanting Entertainments

BY

C. T GANESAN

Published 2005 by arima publishing

www.arimapublishing.com

ISBN 1-84549-027-4

© C. T Ganesan 2005

Printed and bound in the United Kingdom

Typeset in Palatino 11/16

arima publishing
ASK House, Northgate Avenue
Bury St Edmunds, Suffolk IP32 6BB
t: (+44) 01284 700321

www.arimapublishing.com

To my loving granddaughters

Schwetha & Ashvanthi

About this book

1. **What does this book contain?**

   From a glance on the contents one can have an idea of the various topics dealt with in this book. There are numbers of puzzling and sizzling problems solved. Solutions in the form of hints and answers are given at the end of each chapter.

2. **Who should use this book?**

   There is no need for a high level knowledge or technique in Mathematics. But thorough understandings of basic in maths are sufficient. Students who are stuck with "Mathsphobia", allergy to Mathematics are highly recommended to play with this book. The primary purpose of this book is to stimulate or rather to induce interest in principles of Mathematics. Even elders who once studied maths long before can have a past-time study of this book to recollect the forgotten thoughts. Some of the problems can be used for after-dinner jokes. Maths is not a subject of methodical reading but presence of mind and application in wider spectrum of perspective is essential.

3. **How to use this book?**

   Students can attempt few of the problems from this book in between their reading of routine and long passages from literature or boring past events of history. There is no need to study this book from first to last page continuously. At random any page can be opened at any time and read leisurely. Teachers can use this book to select few problems and present to the students to play upon in between their routine lectures which otherwise make them to yawn and sleepy. This may give a short break and rejuvenate their mental alertness.

4. **What recommendations the author can give?**

   The author has more than 36 years of teaching experiences in mathematics to the students in college level. His recommendations are stated below.

   a) Remember that Maths is a skill, just like tennis or swimming. If you do not practice the skill will fade away. So if the ideas in this book are fascinating practice and practice till you become a Maths Magician.

   b) Cultivate the habit of remembering things. Try to remember the birth dates, friends car numbers, e-mail addresses etc. Memorising verses from Bible or slokas from hymns will develop the mind to remember.

   c) Teachers should come down to the level of students, especially when they teach Maths. Teaching Maths is a game like chess played with students. A good teacher may not be a good researcher; but a good researcher can not be good teacher.

d) "A praise of word is better than tons of scolding." Teachers must give plenty of encouragement to the students. When a student shows a sign of improvement do not hesitate to praise him or her. For example, "Many students in higher level can't do this what you are doing now! It is marvellous! Can you solve this mentally? Fantastic! "

e) As a teacher try to avoid the use of calculator. Try to solve as far as possible mentally and accurately. First impression is the best impression.

f) Try to gain the confidence from your students and try to keep it up. Do not show your expertise.

g) Teachers should tell the stories of great Mathematicians and Scientists and inspire them. Who knows, one of your students may be the future Einstein or Newton.

h) Give puzzles and projects to the students as week end assignments. Ask your students to collect similar puzzles from books available in library.

5. **How to inspire confidence in the minds of children?**
   a) Tell them, "It is very easy, you almost got it, and you can do it."
   b) Show with simple examples how they can do it.
   c) Encourage them to join in groups to solve it.
   d) Teacher can also join with them if necessary.
   e) Give them ample chance to think and try again.
   f) Fire their imagination by giving hints.

> *You may think, I have become a lawyer or medical doctor, but you can not live without mathematics because it is part and parcel of every part of everyone's life.*

Prof. C. T. Ganesan

Contents

1.

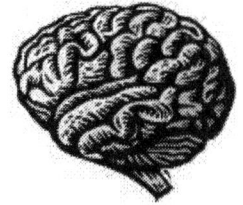

ACTIVE BRAIN CELLS

Ability to remove fixed ideas and to take a wider look for new ones is a trait that is sometimes a great value to the mathematicians.

1. Tubby toasts
Lala roasts tubby toasts in a small pan. After finishing one side she turns it over to other side. Each side takes 30 seconds. The pretty little pan can take only two slices. Help her to toast both sides of three slices exactly in 90 seconds instead of 2 minutes.

2. Mexican problem
When I was going for a walk I found a seven years old boy sitting on a compound wall. He said, " I am the son of the Mexican standing on the ground. We are living in the same house but the person is not my father." Can you guess the actual relationship?

3. Absent minded king
Mr. X got a capital punishment i.e. hanging till he dies. He made an appeal to the King to release him. In the last minute a servant from the King came hurriedly on his horse and gave a letter written on a cloth with a quill pen. The prisoner read the letter and released him even though the king really intended him to be hanged. What was wrong in the letter?

4. Missing one pound
My father, mother and uncle went to a takeaway shop to buy food for the dinner. They decided that each person has to buy same food and to pay individually. So each person bought one large pizza. The cost of each pizza was £10. My father collected money from others and put his share of £10 also and gave £30 to the

bearer who took it to the manager. Manager made a concession and returned £5 to the bearer asking him to return back. The cunning bearer thought wisely how three people could share £5 equally. So he kept £2 in his pocket and returned back £3 which, the three people shared themselves at £1 for each. According to this episode each gave £10 and got back £1, that means each spent £9 and the bearer stole £2. $(3 \times 9) + 2 = £29$. What happened to the remaining £1?

5. Essay competition
There was an essay competition in our class of 28 girls. Schwetha, Sherry, Tia, Camilla, Natasha and Ashvi got the first six places, need not be in the same order and luckily there was not a tie between them. It is quite interesting to note the following result.
Sherry was as many points behind Ashvi as Schwetha was before Camilla.
But the difference between Sherry and Ashvi was more than one.
Schwetha was not first and Ashvi was not fourth and neither Camilla nor Sherry was last.
The number of points of Natasha was half of Tia. Can you find the order of the points the six of them got.

6. Weather forecast
This is a weather forecast for travellers. Now at London it is raining at midnight. I don't know whether it will be a sunny weather after 72 hours at Croydon. Can you help?

7. Taste of the pudding.
Three kinds of puddings are kept in a box. How many puddings must Catherine take to be sure of at least two of them are of same type?
At least three of the puddings are of same type?

8. Grumbling aunt.
"I go one step backward for every two steps forward" cries my aunt in vex. Suppose we consider her statement to be really true, how many steps she will have to make to reach the compound gate which is 20 steps from the main door.

9. Birth day mystery
On a New Year day Jasmine was invited to a party in my house. "Tell me, Jasmine," my Grandpa, began, "I have forgotten the date of your birthday."
After a little thought, Jasmine jokingly replied with the following riddle,
"The day before yesterday I was fifteen, and next year I shall be of age seventeen." What exactly is her birthday and how is her reply sensible?

10. Surgeon refuses

After a car accident a father and a son got severely wounded. When the rescuers took them to hospital, they found that the father was already dead and the boy needed an urgent surgery. There was only one surgeon available in the operation theatre. To the great surprise of all, the surgeon on duty said "I can't do an operation on this boy."

How could it be? What is the relationship between the son and the surgeon?

11. Fathers and sons

In a small village two fathers and two sons left for a pilgrimage and it was found that the population was reduced by three numbers. Assume nobody died and none were born. How could it be?

12. Circus trip

Lora had only £4 in her pocket and she wanted £8 to go to the circus. She said to her mother, "I will bet you, mum for £4 that if you give me eight pounds, I will return back twelve pounds.

The mum accepted immediately. Was the mother wise enough to do so?

13. Grandpa worries about his age.

Transposing my grandpa's age, which is a two-digit number, gives my dad's age. The difference between their ages is twice my sister's age. My dad is 4 times elder than my sister less by one year. What are their ages?

14. Mothers and daughters

Two mothers and two daughters visited my house for a dinner. As a finishing course I wished to give them ice cream. I had only three cones of ice creams. How can I distribute to the guests so that each one of them can have a full cone of ice cream?

15. Forbidden marriage

Have you heard of the man who once married his widow's sister? If you say it is utterly impossible, you are wrong.

16. Confused brothers and sister.

There were two men who were not brothers, but had a common sister. How could it be possible?

17. A cat has seven legs!

One cat has 4 legs and no cat or mathematically speaking 0 cat has three legs. Writing these statements as mathematical equations

1 cat = 4 legs

0 cat = 3 legs and on adding we get 1 cat has 7 legs!

18. £ 1 = 10,000 p

We know the basic algebraic equations like, if $A = X$ and $B = Y$, then $AB = XY$. Similarly,

2 pounds = 200 pennies

$$\frac{1}{2} pound = 50 \, pennies$$

Multiplying the left-hand side and equating to the product of right-hand side we have 1 pound has 10,000 pennies! Do you agree on this transaction?

19. Roundabout trip to Madrid.

A helicopter leaves Madrid and flies straight in north direction for 500 km. Then it makes 90° turn to east and flies another 500 km. Afterwards it again turns 90° to south and flies for 500 km. Finally it turns 90° to westward and makes the last trip for 500 km. Now the question is whether it will land exactly in Madrid airport?

20. Ticket seller's problem.

Mr. Paul is a train ticket seller. He travels in the train itself and sells the ticket. There are 15 stations inclusive of the terminals at start and end of the journey and the train stops at all stations. For a to and fro journey how many kinds of tickets Mr. Paul has to sell?

21. After dinner chat.

Mr. John and his wife are having a chat in front of their house after dinner. John stands at the doorstep and the lady is walking to and fro on the platform. Meanwhile they are counting the pedestrian walkers. Now the question is who is counting more number of people?

22. Childish poet

"Brothers and Sisters have I none,
But that man's father is my father's son"

Do you understand what the poet means?

23. Complicated family
There is a complicated family as stated below.
One Grand father, one grand mother, two fathers, two mothers, four children, three grand children, one brother, two sisters, two sons, two daughters, one father-in-law, one mother-in-law and one daughter-in-law. Totally how many are there in the family? If you say twenty three people you are wrong!

24. Cruising with wolf, goat and cabbage.
This problem can be found in 8th century writings.
A man has to take a wolf, a goat and some cabbage across a river. His rowing boat has enough room for the man and any one of the remaining. Remember that the wolf, meat lover will eat goat and goat will eat the cabbage if they are left without him. Can you give your valuable advice for the man to continue his journey?

25. Interchanging numbers between rows
Write the following each numbers in separate pieces of square papers and place them on a table as shown below. Now ask your friend to replace only two numbers one from each row so that the addition of numbers in each row gives the same value.

$$1 + 2 + 7 + 9 = 19 \qquad \text{row 1}$$

$$3 + 4 + 5 + 8 = 20 \qquad \text{row 2}$$

26. Christmas purchase.
Mr. Parker phoned to his daughter to ask her to buy a few things from supermarket. He told her that she could find enough money in pound notes for the purchase in a sealed envelope inside his desk. She found the envelope with 98 scribbled on the outside of it. In the store she bought £92 worth of things and when she came to the counter to pay she not only didn't have £6 left over but also she was short of money to pay the cashier. Why?

27. Map reading
On a map whose scale is 1: 50,000 a forest is represented by an area of 6 cm². Find in square centimetre the area representing the same forest on a map drawn to a scale of 1: 100.

28. Last name of engine driver.

On the London-Leeds train are there three passengers named as Ganson, Jacob, and Anvar. By coincidence the engine driver, the fireman and the guard have the same last names.

1. Passenger Ganson lives in London

2. The guard lives halfway between London and Leeds.

3. The passenger with the same last name as the guard lives in Leeds.

4. The passenger who lives nearest to the guard earns exactly three times as much as the guard per month.

5. Passenger Jacob earns a pension of £200 a month.

6. Anvar, a member of the crew recently beat the fireman in chess game.

What is the engine driver's last name?

29. Father and his son work in the same factory.

A father and his son live in the same house and they work in the same factory. Father takes 28 minutes to walk to the factory whereas his son takes 20 minutes. Suppose on a day the father leaves home 4 minutes early to his son how long it will take for them to meet each other on their way?

30. Hostel management.

The hostel manager said to the warden, "Three new students, Smith, Griffith and Foster are arriving tomorrow. Their first names are John, Brown and Guard, but not necessarily in that order."

"I think John's last name is Smith." said warden.

"You are wrong", said the manager. "I will give you some hints. The father of Mary Joseph, whom you know well, is the father of Smith's mother. Brown started grade school when he was 7. He wrote me recently, "Finally, this year I am beginning sixth-grade algebra."

The bakery owner, Mr.Samson is Brown's grandfather. Griffith is one year older than Brown and Guard is one year older than Brown.

Give both names and ages of the three boys.

31. Totalling to 100

How many plus marks and where should we put between the digits of 987,654,321 to get a total of 100?

If the total is to be 99 then how many + marks and where will you insert?

32. How many marbles?

Meet your friends A, B and C. Ask A to close your eyes with a black colour cloth. A thinks of a number n, writes it in piece of paper and gives to B of course, without your knowledge. A takes 4n marbles from a basket. B takes 7n and C takes 13n marbles. C gives A and B as many marble as each already has. B does the same to A and C. Finally A does the same to B and C.

Ask one of them how many marbles she has. Divide by 2 and announce how many A took. Divide how many A took by 4, multiply by 7 and this is the amount B took. Divide this answer by 7 and multiply by 13 and announce this as how many C took. But, how will you explain this?

33. Pencil, key and eraser.

For this trick you need three things small enough to hide inside pocket say a small pencil, key and eraser. Keep them on a table and also a plate having 24 marbles. Call your three friends A, B and C. Ask them to take one item per person and hide into their pockets after you leave the room. Then you return back and give one marble to first person whom you like best and two marbles to the next and three marbles to the third. Then tell them. "After I leave the room the person having pencil must take same number of marbles from the plate as I gave to him. The person having key must take twice the number of marbles as much he got from me. The person having eraser must take four times of marbles as much I gave to him." Then you leave the room so that they can do in your absence what you told them. Then you return back and count the number of marbles left on the plate and announce to the great surprise which person is having which item in their pockets.

34. Cricket test match.

Three countries A,B and C played two innings cricket match and points were awarded as detailed below.

10 points for the team that wins.

6 points for the side that wins in the first innings but drawn finally.

2 points for the side that loses in the first innings but the match is drawn.

5 points to each side for a tie.

4 points to each side for a tie in first innings in a drawn match.

0 points to the side that loses.

A, B and C got 12, 6 and 10 points respectively. Find the detailed scores.

35. Peter the wise man

Peter's friend asked why he was very late to return home. Peter said," I had been to shopping where I saw my father's daughter's daughter's only cousin's father. He is a very good and intelligent gentleman."

Who was this remarkable Uncle and where did Peter see him?

36. Age concerned.

"What is your age mum?" asked Tom. "Don't ask the age of a lady and income of a man. It is not of good manners" replied his mother.

"Oh, it's all right," said his uncle. "I am four years younger than your mum. In four years time I shall be four times as old as you are now, and your mum will be three times as old as you will be then!"

How old are Tom, his mum and uncle?

37. Birds in the garden

Mummy was busily baking cookies and Jack was doing homework. Suddenly he called out, "Mum, there are eighteen birds in our garden, and all but six of them flew away. How many birds are still left?"

Twelve, of course", replied his mother. Jack was laughing and harping in to the whole house that mum can't do even the simple subtraction. What was wrong?

38. Cashier and the counterfeit coins.

The cashier of a super market has a little problem. He is having five bags of same number of 10- penny coins. He knew that one of the bag is full of counterfeit coins whereas the remaining four are genuine. Each of genuine coins weighs 50 g and counterfeit coin 40 g. He has an electric weighing machine that allows him to weigh only once. Can you help him to find out which bag holds counterfeit coins?

39. An intelligent old man.

Mark is a land surveyor. Once he was walking in the muddy road of a village where he met an old man who was searching something at the bottom of a big mango tree. As Mark questioned him about this the old man said, "Sir, this is a divine tree. If you put all your money near this root and count up to 100 it will double your money." The surveyor wanted to take his chance and threw his purse closed his eyes and started counting. The old man did something with the purse and returned to the officer who to the great surprise found the money had been doubled.

The villager said, "Every time your money is doubled you have to pay me a commission of £ 1-20p. The greedy surveyor did like this for three times but, Alas! In the last attempt after giving £ 1-20 p there were no money left in his purse. Now the question is how much money the surveyor was initially having in his purse?

40. Green and Red apples

Six closed baskets marked A, B, C, D, E and F contain green and red apples separately with number of fruits indicated. But we don't know which basket contains what colour of apples. Refer to the figure shown below. The fruit seller, Tim says, "If I sell the particular type of basket, I will be having twice the number of red apples left-over than the green apples." Can you find that basket Tim was having in mind before he said this?

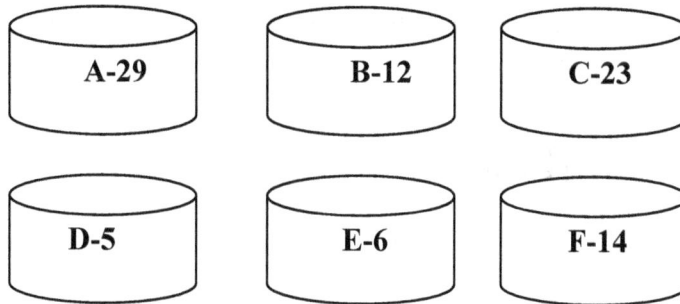

A-29	B-12	C-23
D-5	E-6	F-14

41. Jumbled up socks in the drawer.

In a drawer there are three identical pairs of pink socks, three identical pairs of yellow socks and three identical pairs of green socks. What is the least number of individual socks you have to pull out from the drawer to get a matching pair?

42. Crossing a river by men and women.

Three men and three women need to cross Brent River. They have a boat, but it can only hold two people at a time. Women must never be allowed to outnumber men on either bank. How do they get across the River?

43. A land lord of India.

The land lords in India before independence were called as 'Zamindars'. One such land lord had 17 elephants. He wrote a will that after his death his two sons and one daughter have to share the elephants in the following ratios. Eldest son should receive half of the elephants, the second son gets one third and the daughter must have one ninth of the total he had. The old man died and the confusion started. How to distribute the shares without cutting the elephants! All the three approached the minister who solved the problem wisely. Do you know how the minister distributed the 17 live elephants according to the wish of land lord?

44. Cars in queue.
In a dull afternoon I was watching our street through the window. There were few cars moving slowly one behind the other in a queue. There were four cars in front and four cars behind and three cars in the middle. Still when counted the number of cars it was fewer than half a dozen! What was wrong?

45. Species collection.
Balan is very happy in collecting different species of creatures. Once he had some birds, spiders and bees. There were in total 19 of them with 72 legs. Can you find how many in each variety he had?

46. Maths and physics competition.
Every year our school used to give award for the best five students in the form VI examination in the subjects maths and physics. The prize award committee for this year has announced the following results.
a) Bernard is as many places above Daniel in maths as Daniel is above Bernard in physics. But neither of them secured first place in maths and physics.
b) Emily is below Bernard in physics and Bernard is above Emily in maths.
c) Ashvi is less mathematical than Schwetha and Schwetha is less in physics than Ashvi.
d) Emily secured neither the lowest in maths nor in physics.
Put them in the order of their merit.

47. Sports competition.
Alex, Balle, Charlie, Doe and Elias took part in the annual sports activities. Alex scored points as many places above Balle as Doe was above Elias. Neither Charlie nor Elias was third or fifth. Find the rank of their points scored.

48. Flower bunch.
In a flower bunch there were 21 flowers of yellow and red colours mixed. Yellow flowers were having 5 petals whereas the red flowers were of 7 petals. When only the petals were counted they were 121. How many flowers were yellow coloured?

49. An ancient Roman problem.
A Roman Lord at his death bed made a will in the presence of his attorney and died. At that time his wife was pregnant. According to his will if the lady gives birth to a son the boy will get two third of his estate .and the widow will have one

third. Otherwise if the lady gives birth to a girl the daughter will get one third and the widow will get two third.

Man proposes and God disposes! The widow had given birth to twins, a boy and a girl. What sharing of estate will be as closely agreeable as possible to the will?

50. Left-hand cricket player.
A left hand cricket player was drinking tea during tea-break in a nicely decorated tea-cup. Which side of the cup will be the handle? Of course he was holding the cup in his left hand.

51. Grandpa and grand son.
"In the year 1938 my age was half of the last two digits of 1938" I told this to my grandfather. Immediately he replied, "The same condition agrees to my age also". I was wondering how my age and my grandpa's age who is walking with walking stick could be the same! Then what exactly were our ages in 1938?

52. School clubs and activities.
In our school there are five non academic clubs. They are politics club, literature society, photography club, chess players club and music club. They meet according to the following schedule.

Politics club	Every alternate day
Literature society	Every third day
Photography club	Every fourth day
Chess club	Every fifth day
Music club	Every sixth day

All these five clubs met for the first time on January 1st 2005. Even during government holidays or any other public holidays they met according to the schedule.

Leaving the first meeting when will all the five clubs meet on the same day within the first quarter i.e. 90 days of 2005?

Within the first 90 days how many days none of the clubs met?

53. Deceiving sledge dogs.
Dr. Yakov from Arctic Polar Regions tells his experience. Once he was travelling from his hospital to military camp to attend a serious patient. His sledge was pulled by five huskies at a constant full speed for 24 hours. Then suddenly two dogs ran off and disappeared. Dr. Yakov had to travel the remaining distance

with only three dogs and his speed of travel was lowered proportionately. He reached the camp 48 hours later than he had planned. If the runaway dogs were stayed for 80 more kms, he would have been only 24 hours late. How far is the military camp from doctor's hospital?

54. Broken bracelet.

Mr. Fraser brought five pieces gold chains to a goldsmith. Each piece had three links Mr. Fraser wanted them to be connected to one full length with a hook so that he can use it as a bracelet. The goldsmith was about to break one of the end link from each of four pieces in order to connect to the fifth piece. Fraser's little son who was seeing this suggested, "Don't break the four links and waste the gold, just break three links only!"; but what was his idea?

55. Cake for the party.

Miss. Forget broke all the eggs from a small basket to beat with sugar to make a large size cake. But she always forgets and now also she forgot. She asked her brother, "Tony, do you remember how many eggs you bought today?"

"If you put in groups of three at a time one will remain. If you put in groups of four at a time again one will be left over. But if you select in groups of five at a time nothing will remain." Tony told this riddle and ran over to play. How many eggs Tony bought from market and kept in the *small* basket?

56. An old riddle of thirty one legs.

Two legs was sitting on three legs holding one leg. At that time six legs visited through the open window and sat over the one leg. Also four legs came and pinched the one leg. The two legs got wild, picked the three legs and threw at the four legs who dropped the one leg and ran away. The two legs went and picked up the one leg and ate it happily. Can you solve this riddle?

Answers: Active Brain Cells

1. Let us name the slices as A, B, C. First she puts A and B on the pan and toasts one side. It takes first 30 seconds. She removes B, turns A to other side and also puts C on the pan. After the next 30 seconds she removes A, which is fully done, turns C to other side and puts B back to the pan to toast other back. At the end of third 30 seconds she gets all the three slices ready. So it took on the whole 90 seconds only!

2. The answer is mother.

3. The king wrote like this. "HANG HIM NOT. RELEASE HIM." Actually the king forgot to put a full stop after the words HANG HIM! Instead he wrongly put a full stop after NOT.

4. This episode is stated in a tricky way to drag your mind in a wrong direction. In fact each of the three spent £8.33 and totally they spent 3 x 8.33 = £25, bearer took £2 and they got £3 back that amounts to £30.

5. Answer: First - Ashvi, Schwetha - second, Natasha – third, Sherry – fourth, Camilla – fifth, Tia – sixth.

6. No, it will be midnight!

7. 4 puddings, 7 puddings

8. 58 steps

9. 30th December.

10. Mother.

11. Grandfather, father and son.

12. No. Lora took eight pounds from mum and simply walked out. Her mum cried, "Hey, you lost your bet, you don't give twelve pounds." Lora turned back and said, "Sorry mum. It is true that I lost the bet and take the money for loosing the bet, £4." She gave back £4 according to her bet and enjoyed the circus too!

13. The difference of any two transposed numbers is a multiple of 9. This can be any thing from 0 to 72. i.e. (11 –11) to (91 –19). Hence sister's age is half of 18. The ages are 53, 35 and 9 respectively. Check: 4 X 9 – 1 = 35

14. Grandmother, mother and daughter.

15. The man say Mr. John was young and he married Anna. A few years later the man married Anna's sister also with the consent of Anna. After few years Mr. John died and Anna became a widow. So he married his widow's sister.

16.   Mrs. A + Mr. A = Son of AA
         Mrs. B + Mr. C = Son of BC
         Mrs. B + Mr. A = Daughter of AB
Son AA and son BC are unrelated and they don't have common genes. But still they are the brothers of the girl AB!

17. Misunderstanding of the axiom of 'zero'.

18. Multiplication gives the square of pounds and squares of pennies.

19. The route is not a perfect square shape because of the three dimensional plane and due to the spherical shape of earth. The lines of latitude and longitude make it to be a sort of spherical- square short by 77 km on the east.

20. 14 x 15 = 210 types of tickets.

21. Same number.

22. As he says the poet is the only child, then 'my father's son' is the speaker himself. And so he is his father's son!

23. They are only seven but it is with 23 relationships. If you workout carefully with patience you will get the result.

24. He takes first the goat only to other side and leaves it there by tying its legs. He returns back.
Second trip he takes cabbage to the other shore, leaves the cabbage and brings back the goat.
Third trip he takes the wolf and leaves it on the other side with cabbage and comes back to take the goat across. Thus he crosses the river seven times.

25. Move 8 from row 2 to row 1 in place of 9. Rotate '9' by 180° and move down to the place of 8.

26. She unfortunately read 86 as 98.

27. 1.5 cm^2

28. Jacob is not the person living nearest to the guard since £200 is too low and if this is true guard's pay can not be £66.67 per month. (4-5). By 1 Ganson is eliminated. So he is Anvar. Since the passenger from Leeds is not Ganson he must be Jacob. Since Anvar is not the fireman (6), he is the engine driver!

29. 10 minutes.

30. Smith's grandfather is Joseph and Brown's grandfather is Samson. Hence Smith is not Brown. Griffith is not Brown. So Brown must be Foster. By elimination John is Griffith. Since Brown started first grade at 7 now he must be 12 because he is now in 6th grade. The other two boys are 13.
Guard Smith is 13 years. John Griffith is also 13 and Brown Foster is 12 years.

31. $9 + 8 + 7 + 65 + 4 + 3 + 2 + 1 = 99$ also $9 + 8 + 7 + 6 + 5 + 43 + 21 = 99$.
If it is for 100 then $1 + 2 + 34 + 56 + 7 = 100$ and $1 + 23 + 4 + 5 + 67 = 100$

32.

	A	B	C
Initially	4n	7n	13n
After first step	8n	14n	2n
After second step	16n	4n	4n
After third step	8n	8n	8n

33.

B	A	C
k	p	e
e	p	k
p	k	e
e	k	p
p	e	k
k	e	p

The table shows the account of marbles taken and balance remaining in the plate. It can be seen that the remnants of marbles are different in each case. Copy these two tables in a notebook and keep it in the other room. Let your friends are not aware of these tables. After counting the balance of marbles go back to the other room and refer to the tables. Suppose there are only five marbles in the plate refer to the table shown below It is 'k,e,p'. So A has the key, B has eraser and C has pencil. If you want to be successful you have to remember how many marbles you have given which person so that you can identify who is A,B or C.

ABC	Account of marbles	Total	Balance
pke	1+1=2; 2+4=6; 3+12=15	23	1
pek	1+1=2; 2+8=10; 3+6=9	21	3
kpe	1+2=3; 2+2=4; 3+12=15	22	2
kep	1+2=3; 2+8=10; 3+3=6	19	5
epk	1+4=5; 2+2=4; 3+6=9	18	6
ekp	1+4=5; 2+4=6; 3+3=6	17	7

34. This is worked with logical trials. For the match, A with B, B won on first innings but the match was drawn. So B got 6 and A got 2. For the match A versus C, A won and got 10, C got 0. In the match B versus C, B lost C won with 10 points.

35. Peter himself. Peter's father's daughter's daughter is Peter's sister's daughter otherwise his niece. So Peter is her uncle. Her only cousin's father is her only uncle. Hence Peter must be her only uncle. He saw himself standing before a mirror.

36. 8, 32 and 28 years respectively

37. This is actually a puzzle in English. "All but six of them" means except six the other 12 flew away!

38. First he has to keep five bags in a line and has to number them to identify. He takes one coin from first bag, two coins from second bag, three from third bag, four from fourth bag and five from fifth bag and puts on the balance of the weighing machine. Now there are 15 coins and they and surely they will not weigh 750 g which is the correct weight if all the coins were genuine. The difference will be in multiples of 10 g. Suppose the machine shows 710 g, the fourth bag is of counterfeit coins.

39. Assume £x as the initial money and try to form equation. He had £ 1 – 05p initially in his purse.

40. Tim was thinking of basket marked 'A'. Baskets B, C and D have red apples.

41. At least four socks have to be pulled out.

42. A man and a lady cross the river first. The man returns alone. Then two ladies now cross and one of the lady returns. Now two men cross. One man and one woman return. Two men cross and one woman returns. Finally the remaining two women cross.

43. The wise minister added his own elephant in to the group. So the total number had become 18 so that 18 can be easily and as wholesome be divided in the ratio as stated in the will. Hence elder son got 9, second son got 6 and the daughter got 2 elephants totalling to 17. The remaining one, the minister's own elephant was taken back by him.

44. Nothing was wrong. See the figure below.

$$\longrightarrow \quad \boxed{E} \quad \boxed{D} \quad \boxed{C} \quad \boxed{B} \quad \boxed{A} \quad \longrightarrow$$

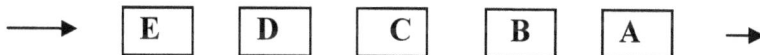

Cars A, B, C, D are in front while E is behind or Cars B, C, D, E are at the back with car A in front or Cars B, C, D are in the middle of A and E. Altogether there were five cars.

45. You must be aware that spider has 8 legs and bee has 6 legs. He had 12 birds, 3 spiders and 4 bees.

46. According to the statements a, b, c, and d, the following table can be prepared. The names of the pupil are given in alphabets.

Maths: 1. Schwetha, 2. Bernard, 3. Daniel, 4. Emily, 5. Ashvi
Physics: 1. Ashvi, 2. Daniel, 3. Bernard, 4. Emily, 5. Schwetha.

Order	Maths	Physics
1	S	A
2	B A S	D S A
3	B D E A S	D B S A
4	D E A S	D B E S A
5	D A	B S

47. Charlie, Doe, Alex, Elias and Balle.

48. The total petals = 121 = (13 x 5) + (8 x 7). Therefore the answer is 13 numbers of yellow flowers with each 5 petals.

49. There is no single compromising answer to this problem.
One Roman Jurist, Salvian Julian proposed the following. The father's intention was clearly the daughter should receive half as much as her mother, the son twice the share of his mother. Hence Mother:daughter:son = 2:1:4.
An opposing view. The father's wish was that the mother should get at least one third. But Salivan's proposal is two seventh to mother which is not justifiable. Hence the mother should get one third and the rest two third must be divided as before in the ratio 1:4 for daughter and son. As per this the mother gets 5 parts, the daughter gets 2 and son gets 8 parts.
Russian's proposal: Because the birth was twins one of them would have born first. If it was girl first she will be entitled one third of the estate and if it was boy first, he will have two third and the rest will go to mother.

50. Nothing to do with Maths. It's just to tickle your brain cells! The handle will be out side of the cup!

51. It is evident from the statement of the problem that the grand son was born in 20th century and the grand father was born on 19th century. Half of 38 is 19

and so G. Son was born in 1919 and his age in 1938 was 19. Twice 69 is 138. Hence G. Father's year of birth is 1869 and his age in 1938 was 69.

52. Year 2005 is not a leap year. The least common multiple of 2, 3, 4, 5 and 6 is 60. Hence on the 61st day, March 2nd they all meet. For the second part of the question one has to patiently write numbers 1, 2, 3, 4, 5… ..up to 90. Cancel out the days on which they can not meet. You may find totally for 24 days during the first 90 days they could not meet.

53. If the doctor covered 80 more km at full speed he would have reached the camp one day earlier otherwise if he had covered 160 km with all the 5 dogs at full speed he would have reached the camp as planned. Therefore 160 km were remaining to reach the camp after the two dogs ran away at the end of first day. With 5 dogs at full speed he would have covered more than 160 km. i.e. 160 x 5/3 = 266.7 km. Not travelling this extra 106.7 km could have saved him 48 hours as the problem says. Full speed then was 53.35 km per day. So he travelled 53.35 km for the first day with 5 dogs and 160 km with three dogs. Hence the distance was 213.35 km which he travelled in 4 days instead of two days as he had planned earlier.

54. Each time when cutting a link some amount of gold may be wasted in the form of powder. His idea was to cut three links from one piece and use them to connect the remaining four pieces.

55. It can be 25, 49 or 73 etc. Since it is stated as small basket the number of eggs must be 25.

56. A lady was sitting on a three legged stool eating the honey-roasted leg of a chicken. Through the open window a bee entered and sat on the roasted leg to taste the honey. Her naughty dog also came and pinched the chicken leg. She took the tripod and threw at the dog who dropped the chicken leg. She went and took back the leg and ate it happily and threw the bone to her dog.

2.

ACROBATIC ALGEBRA

Algebra is generous; she often gives more than is asked of her.

D' Alembert.

1. Any number equals to any other number; otherwise any number is equal to zero.

Let $a = b$, then by multiplying by 'a' on both sides we get $a^2 = ab$
Subtracting b^2 on both sides, we have
$a^2 - b^2 = ab - b^2 = b(a - b)$,
$(a - b)(a + b) = b(a - b)$,
Cancelling $(a - b)$ on both sides, we have $(a + b) = b$.
Suppose $a = 3$, $b = 3$ in the above proved equation. Then $6 = 3$
Also from $(a + b) = b$, since we assumed $a = b$ it becomes $2b = b$ or $2 = 1$!
From the equation $(a + b) = b$ subtracting b from both sides we get $a = 0$, otherwise any number equals to 'zero'. Very funny!

2. Funny equations!
a) $(-a)^2 = (+a)^2$ extracting square root on both sides
$-a = +a$
b)   £ ¼ = 25 p extracting square root we get
£ ½ = 5p.
c)   Consider the two equations,
$1 \times 0 = 2 \times 0$ and $0 = 0$. Dividing these two equations we get $1 = 2$

3. Drunkard's intelligence.

A man is accused by his indignant wife of having too much of drinks. He managed his mathematically talented wife this way.

½ full glass of whisky = ½ empty glass

Multiplying by 2 on either side we get

1 full glass of whisky = 1 empty glass, so no need to worry!

4.　To prove that any two unequal numbers are equal.

Let a = b + c, multiply with (a – b) on both sides.

Then, a (a – b) = (b +c) (a – b)

$$a^2 – ab = ab + ac – b^2 – bc$$
$$a^2 – ab – ac = ab – bc – b^2$$
$$a (a – b – c) = b(a – b – c),$$ cancelling (a – b – c) we have a = b.

5.　To prove that all positive whole numbers are equal.

$$\left(\frac{x-1}{x-1}\right) = 1$$

$$\left(\frac{x^2 - 1}{x - 1}\right) = x + 1$$

$$\left(\frac{x^3 - 1}{x - 1}\right) = x^2 + x + 1$$

$$\left(\frac{x^4 - 1}{x - 1}\right) = x^3 + x^2 + x + 1$$

By long division we have the above stated identities.

Like this we can also have for the nth term

$$\left(\frac{x^n - 1}{x - 1}\right) = x^{n-1} + x^{n-2} + \dots\dots x^2 + x + 1$$

In all these equations if we substitute x = 1, we get

$$\frac{0}{0} = 1 = 2 = 3 = 4 = \dots\dots = n$$

6. Jerome Cordon's method to solve cubical equation of the form $x^3 + px = q$

Substitute $x = u - v$, such that $uv = p/3$. Let us take an example of solving
$x^3 + 6x - 20 = 0$, note that $p = 6$, and $q = 20$
$(u - v)^3 + 6(u - v) = 20$
$u^3 - 3u^2v + 3uv^2 - v^3 + 6(u - v) = 20$
$(u^3 - v^3) - 3uv(u - v) + 6(u - v) = 20$, substituting $uv = p/3 = 2$, $(u^3 - v^3) = 20$, but uv
$= 2$ and $v = 2/u$, therefore,

    $u^3 - 8/u^3 = 20$
    $u^6 - 20u^3 - 8 = 0$ put $u^3 = a$
    $a^2 - 20a - 8 = 0$ which solves as $a = u^3 = 20.4$
    $u = 2.73$ and $v = 0.73$ therefore $x = u - v = 2$

7. Typist Priya

Miss Priya promised to her boss that she can type at the rate of 20 pages a day. She typed the first half of the manuscript lazily at 10 pages a day and for the second half she hurried at 30 pages a day to make up the delay thinking that the average of rates of typing 10 and 30 is equal to 20. Is Priya correct in her assumptions?

8. Crossing goods trains

Two goods trains each 1/6 km long travelling in opposite direction at 60 km per hour meet and pass each other. How many seconds left between after the engines passing each other and the guard's van at the end pass each other?

9. Time and distance

The average speed of the first third of a journey was two- third of the average speed over the remaining distance. If the journey took 7 hours all together, how long did the first third journey took place?

10. Filling a bath tub.

A bathtub takes 4 minutes to get filled up fully and it takes 5 minutes to get drained completely. The tub is already half full with hot water. How long will it take to fill the tub while both the tap and drain are fully opened?

11. Diluted alcohol

How many litres of 15% alcohol must be added to 1000 litres of 98 % alcohol to obtain 90 % of alcohol?

12. Mosquito challenges with an elephant!

Once the Mosqui, mosquito challenged with Jumbo that weights of both of them are the same. Let us see how the smart mosquito argued his statement.

Let x be the weight of the elephant and y that of the mosquito. Call the sum of these two weights as 2a, then

$x + y = 2a$, this equation results

$x = - y + 2a$ and $x - 2a = - y$, multiplying these two equations we get

$x^2 - 2ax = y^2 - 2ay$, adding a^2 to both sides

$x^2 - 2ax + a^2 = y^2 - 2ay + a^2$

$(x - a)^2 = (y - a)^2$ taking back the square root

$(x - a) = (y - a)$. Cancelling a on both sides, we get $x = y$, that is to say that the weight of the mosquito is same as that of the Jumbo elephant! Can you wipe away the tears of dear Jumbo and keep up his prestige?

13. Stationery shopping with friends.

Three friends Daniel, Schwetha and Ashvanthi went to a stationery shop. Daniel purchased 4 pens, an eraser and 10 pencils for £1.69. Schwetha bought 3 pens, an eraser and 7 pencils and paid £1.26. If our dear Ashvanthi had bought only one of each how much she has to pay?

14. Stunning simultaneous equation

Can you solve these equations simultaneously in your head?

$6,751x + 3,249y = 26,751$
$3,249x + 6,751y = 23,249$

15. Crazy candles

Two candles blue and red colour have different lengths and thicknesses. The long, blue candle can burn for 4 hours and short, red candle for 7 hours. After burning for 2 ½ hours the candles were of same lengths. What was the ratio of heights of the candles originally?

16. Set up your watch correctly.

My watch is 1 second fast per hour and Ashvi's watch is one and half second slow per hour. Right now they show the same time. (a) When will they show the same time again? (b) When will they show the same *correct* time again?

17. Considerate MCQ test.

On a 40 numbers of Multiple Choice Questions test, five marks were deducted for every wrong answer and 15 marks were credited for every right answer. If a candidate obtained zero mark how many wrong answers were there?

18. Candle bonus

A lady entered a store and bought x candles for y pounds. When she was about to pay money the cashier said to her, "If you buy ten more candles I will give you all for £2, and thereby you will save 80 cents a dozen". Find x and y which are integers.

19. Here is a great offer to the readers.

In this bag there are plenty of 50 pence, 20 pence and 5 pence coins. Select exactly twenty numbers of coins from this bag and make £5 and give it to me. Then I promise that I will give you £50. How can you miss this great opportunity?

20. Cash problems

From the above problem show that it is not possible to make £3 or £2 with the combination of 50p, 20p and 5p totally numbering to 20 coins.

21. Five unknowns to solve!

Solve the following set of simultaneous equations without struggling too much!

$a + c + d + e = 5$
$a + b + d + e = 1$
$a + b + c + e = 2$
$a + b + c + d = 0$
$b + c + d + e = 4$

22. Row Row Row the boat.

Jasmin rows on a river, x km with the current and x km against the current. Her brother rows 2x km on a lake where the water is still. Does Jasmin takes more or less time than her brother?

23. Fox hunting.

Three friends A, B and C started from London for fox hunting. On their way they had to cross a river and the case containing cartridges of A and B got wet and useless. So they had to share equally from what C was having. After each had fired 4 shots, the total cartridges remaining were equal to the number each had before the division. How many cartridges C was having in the beginning?

24. Three lazy boys.

Four boys, A, B, C, D and their sister, E went for collecting straw-berries. But the lazy boys were sleeping nicely under the shade of a tree while the girl collected 45 fruits. The sister was feeling sympathetic and didn't like the boys to return home empty handed. She distributed each boy some fruits and had nothing for her self. On the way back A had 2 fruits and C had twice the number of fruits he already had. But the boys B and D were fooling around all the way. As a result of this B lost 2 fruits and D lost half of his fruits.

When they reached home their mother counted and found all the boys had equal number of fruits and the girl none. How many fruits the sister gave to each of her brothers?

25. A smart little sister

Three sisters shared 24 apples between them each getting a number equal to their ages 3 years before. The youngest one proposed a swap,

"I will keep only half the apples I got and the rest I will divide equally between the middle and elder sister. The middle sister must keep half of the accumulated apples to herself and the other half she has to distribute equally between the eldest sister and me. Now the eldest sister has to distribute half of her accumulated apples to me and to the middle sister."

They all agreed to this proposal but to their surprise in the end they all had equally 8 apples. How old were the sisters?

26. Walking and running

Two athletes A and B have been asked to cover the same distance and reach the goal post. A runs half the time and walks the second half of time. B runs halfway and walks the rest of distance. Neither one runs or walks faster than the other. Who gets to the destination first? If they walked and then ran, who would get to the post first?

27. Clocks, clocks everywhere!

In my room I have a wall clock, a table clock and an alarm clock. I always wear my wristwatch also. But none of them are showing accurate time! The wall clock loses 100 seconds an hour. The table clock gets 100 seconds ahead of the wall clock. The alarm clock runs 100 seconds behind the table clock. The pity is even my wristwatch is 100 seconds ahead of alarm clock. At midnight I set all the four timepieces correct and went to sleep. When I got up from bed and looked at the time shown by the BBC news as 7 AM what would have been the time shown by each of my wonderful timepieces?

28. Fast and slow cars.

Two cars make a journey of 360 km. The average speed of one car is 20 km/h more than the other car. They start the journey at the same time. The faster one reaches the destination 36 minutes ahead of the second car. What are the speeds of the two cars?

29. Marathon runners

Tom runs 2 km and George runs 4 km. Tom's average speed is 10 km/h less than that of George. Tom's running time is 5 minutes more than that of George. Find the speed of each person.

30. Brain sharpener.

Two police boats travel across a big lake with constant but not equal speeds. Boat M leaves shore A and at the same time boat N leaves the opposite shore B. They meet for the first time at a distance 700 m from A. Each returns from their opposite shores without halting, and they meet 500 m from B. How long is the lake and how the two boats' speeds are related?

31. Wealth dreamers.

A wealthy old lady adopted two sons who have become vagabond and spendthrifts. At the time of her death she made a will and left it with her lawyer. The sons somehow knew the total value of the money but they do not know how much each is going to get. The first boy said, "If the will is favourable to me I will have twice as much as in my account at the bank." The second boy started dreaming by saying, "No, mum has written the complete lot on my name only. I am going to have three times my present savings in the bank." But to their great disappointment the old lady has written the will in favour of charity. The vexed brothers combined their own savings which amounted to £ 12,000 to start a business. What was the amount in the will the old lady had written?

32. Promise for salary increase.

"I will agree to increase your salary" said the manager to Mr. Smith, "but there are two choices and you have to select one of them." Mr. Smith agreed to this.
Manager continued, "I will increase you salary by one-third and in addition you will get £ 100 per week. The alternate proposal is your salary will be increased by one quarter with an addition of £ 150 per week."
Mr. Smith thought for a while and said, "Sir, both of your proposals will bear the same benefit to me. So you may grant any one of them." If that is so what was Mr. Smith original salary per week before the increase?

33. A sweet purchase

Mrs. Thomas purchased some sugar for £2.16 for cake making. Had the sugar price reduced by three pennies for one kilo gram she would have received 1 kg more for the same expenditure. How many kilo grams of sugar did she buy?

34. Factorising a giant number.

Find the prime factors of 1,000,027

35. The train and two observers.

Seenu said, "The goods train passes me in 30 seconds." His sister Usha said, "It passed the Elliot's bridge which is 750 metres long in one minute and twenty seconds."

The train was travelling in uniform speed. What was its speed and how long it was?

36. Consistent equations.

For what value of k in the following simultaneous equations are to be consistent?

$x + y = 2$

$kx + y = 4$

$x + ky = 6$

37. Red Riding Hood cycles to her Aunt's house.

If Red riding hood pedals her cycle at the rate of 10kmph she can reach her aunt's house at 1pm. If she goes at 15kmph she can reach at 11am itself. But if she wants to reach her aunt's house exactly at 12 noon at what speed she has to travel?

38. Two typists.

Mr. Max who is an experienced typist takes two hours to finish the job of typing a report. Miss. Julie who is less experienced takes three hours to complete the same job. If both of them share the job equally how long they will take to finish typing the report?

39. Age of a mathemagician.

We asked the age of Mr. James who is interested always in maths puzzles. "Multiply my age after three years by three and take away from that three times my age earlier by three years. Then you will get my present age." This was his brain twisting reply. What is his present age?

40. Making fruit juice.

A cup (A) with concentrated lemon syrup and another cup (B) of pure water of same weight are on the table.

My mother took 20 gm of syrup from A and mixed with water in the second cup B. Then she took two third of this mixture from B and poured in to the first cup A of pure syrup and thoroughly mixed.

Now the mixture in cup A is four times of weight of mixture in the cup B. Find out how much of syrup and water were initially taken.

41. Spending in supermarket.

I took approximately £15 to the supermarket. The money was in the denomination of certain amount of one pound coins and some 20 pence coins.

After shopping when returned back I checked the balance and found the number of one pound coins in my pocket were equal to the number of 20p coins I took to the market and the number of 20p coins in my pocket were equal to the number of one pound coins I took.

When counted the balance it was one third of the money I took to the supermarket. How much exactly I spent?

42 Xmas bonanza

Rita and Ramesh are sister and brother, Rita being elder to Ramesh she used to get more. Their father used to give them pocket money every week. The sum of their pocket money is £32 and the product is 240.

Just before Christmas father wanted to surprise them by increasing in total the pocket money by £24 more but in the inverse ratio of what they were getting before.

What was the exact money they got on the eve of Christmas?

43. Ages of three friends.

Mary, Seetha and Fathima are friends studying in primary class. Mary is the youngest and Fathima is the eldest. If their ages can be assumed as x, y, and z then

$x + y + z = 21$,

$xy + yz + zx = 146$ and $xyz = 336$. Find their ages.

44. Distinction in Maths.

Shanthi was very happy on that evening. Her father asked about her marks in the maths examination. She gave her reply in the form of a puzzle.

"One third of my mark multiplied with one seventh of my mark is equal to four times my mark!" What exactly is her mark?

45. Mrs. Gibbon's age.

When her son was born, Mrs. Gibbon was two fifth of her father's age. After certain years her son was one third of her age and her father was twice her age. At that time the total of all their ages was 100 years.

What was the age of Mrs. Gibbon when her son was born?

46. Guitar music shop

A music shop has a number of six stringed guitars and four stringed guitars totalling to 60 guitars all together. The total number strings when counted for both type of guitars came to 326. How many six stringed guitars are in stock?

47. Sisters' ages.

Find the ages of the two sisters satisfying the following peculiar conditions. The difference of their ages is 5 and at the same time the age of elder sister is five times that of younger one!

48. Ranks in the class.

Ram, Rahim, Sheela and Shalini are the first four rank winners in the class; but not in the same order. If their ranks are represented by x, y, z and w respectively satisfying the following conditions find their ranks.

$$x + y + z + w = 10 \ldots \ldots \qquad \ldots \qquad (1)$$
$$x^2 + y^2 + z^2 + w^2 = 30 \ldots \qquad \ldots \qquad (2)$$
$$x^3 + y^3 + z^3 + w^3 = 100 \ldots \qquad \ldots \qquad (3)$$
$$xyzw = 24 \text{ and } w > x > y > z.. \qquad (4)$$

49. Who drove the motor-cycle?

One day Mr. Peterson and his daughter left the village to visit the city. One was riding on the horse and the other was driving a motor-cycle. Soon it became apparent to them that if the father had ridden four times as far as he had, he would have three-fourth as far to ride as he had. If the daughter had ridden one third as she had, she would have three times as far to ride as she had. Who rode the horse and who drove the motor-cycle?

50. Impossible ages.

There are two daughters for Mrs. Fumi. If the ages of two daughters are represented as 'a' and 'b' and it is found that $\left[\dfrac{a}{b} + \dfrac{b}{a}\right]$ is an integer. What are their ages?

51. Linear simultaneous equations of four unknowns.

Solve the following simultaneous equations without tears!

$$x + 6y + 4v + 3u = 12 \ldots \quad \ldots \quad (1)$$
$$7x + 5y + 8v + 2u = -12 \ldots \quad \ldots \quad (2)$$
$$2x + 8y + 5v + 7u = 12 \ldots \quad \ldots \quad (3)$$
$$3x + 4y + 6v + u = -12 \ldots \quad \ldots \quad (4)$$

52. Unexpected guests.

Mr. Harish wanted to distribute £24 to his children to spend during their picnic party. Two of their cousins joined in the last moment unexpectedly. Mr. Harish is not prepared to spend more than £24. Hence each child got 60p less than what they would have got according to original plan. How many children attended the party?

Rene Descartes (1596 – 1650). He was the contemporary of Galileo. Apart from being a soldier he discovered the idea of 'cartesian' geometry before his battle in Prague. The word 'cartesian' was derived from his name and his work bridged a link between geometry and algebra which inevitably led to discovery of calculus. He finally settled in Holland for ten years. Later he moved to Sweden where he died of pneumonia.

Answers: Acrobatic Algebra

1. Assuming a = b is not correct

2. a) 0/0 is indeterminate
b)   Square root of a² is +a or –a
c)   While extracting square root we have to do that for '£' and 'p' also.

4. The division of 0 by 0 is indeterminate.

5. 0/0 is undefined.

7. No. Priya is wrong. Assuming total number of pages as 'n' she can complete the work in n/20 days. But she actually takes $\dfrac{n}{20} + \dfrac{n}{60} = \dfrac{n}{15}$ days. Because of this delay she takes $\dfrac{n}{15} - \dfrac{n}{20} = \dfrac{n}{60}$ more days than promised.

8. When the engines just cross the guards compartments are at $1/6 + 1/6 = 1/3$ km apart. It will take 20 seconds.

9. The distance ratio is 1 : 2; the speed ratio is 2 : 3. Dividing these two we get the time ratio as 3 : 4. Therefore the first part of journey takes in 3 hours.

10. When the drain tap is closed and filling tap opened in one minute ¼ th tub is filled. When drain tap is opened and filling tap is closed in one minute 1/5 tub is drained. But the tub is already half-full and both the taps are opened. In one minute $\dfrac{1}{4} - \dfrac{1}{5} = \dfrac{1}{20}$.part of the tub is filled. Hence to fill the remaining half portion of the tub it will take 10 minutes.

11. Assume that 'x' litres of 15% alcohol to be added. Hence pure alcohol added is 0.15 x litres. Already pure alcohol content in 1000 litres is 980 litres. Hence (980 + 0.15x) litres of pure alcohol are contained in (1000 + x) litres of mixture. Hence $\dfrac{980 + 0.15x}{1000 + x} = \dfrac{90}{100}$. Solve for x. 106.67 litres to be added.

12. The square root of (y – a)² can also be –(y – a)!

13. $4x + y + 10z = 169..$ ..   ..   (1)
         $3x + y + 7z = 126..$ ..   ..   (2)
$2(1) - 3(2)$ will give you $x + y + z = 40p$ which Ashvanthi had to pay

14   Add and subtract mentally and you may get some idea!

15. Long candle's length is x and short is y. After 2½ hours 5x/8 of long candle is burnt and 3x/8 is remaining; 5y/14 of short candle is burnt and 9y/14 is remaining. $\dfrac{3}{8}x = \dfrac{9}{14}y$ and x/y = 12/7. The short, red candle is 7/12 of longer, blue one.

16. Both watches will show same time when gain of my watch is equal to the loss of time of Ashvi's watch i.e. in 12 hours gap. (43,200 secs.). In x hours my watch will gain x secs. and Ashvi's watch will lose 1.5x secs.
$x + 1.5x = 43,200$
$x = 17,280$ hours or 720 days.
Answer for the second part will be still more difficult. The correct time will be shown by both watches until mine is a multiple of 12 hours fast and her watch is in multiples of 12 hours slow. This will happen to my watch in 43,200 secs. i.e. 1800 days and for Ashvi's watch 1800 x 2/3 = 1200 days. The common multiple of these two is 3,600 days.

17. 30 questions were answered wrongly.

18. Since y is an integer and less than 2, y = 1. $\dfrac{100}{x} - \dfrac{200}{x+10} = \dfrac{80}{12}$ or $x^2 + 25x -$
$150 = 0$ and $x = 5$
She bought 5 candles for £1.

19. $50x + 20y + 5z = 500$, dividing by 5, we get
$10x + 4y + z = 100$. Equation for coins will be
$x + y + z = 20$. Eliminating z from these two equations we get $3x + y = 26\dfrac{2}{3}$, 3x
is three numbers of 50 penny coins and y is twenty penny coin and sum can not be a fraction and doesn't make a sense.

21. Add all the five equations and divide by 4 to get a + b + c + d + e = 3. Now subtract each of the five equations from this to get a = -1, b = -2, c = 2, d = 1 and e = 3.

22. Some will jump into conclusion that they will take same time. That is wrong. Time taken by Jasmin is

$$\frac{x}{r+c} + \frac{x}{r-c} = \frac{2xr}{r^2 - c^2}$$ where r is the speed in still water and c is the speed of current.

Time taken by her brother is $\frac{2x}{r}$. Divide the two timings

$$\frac{time\ taken\ by\ Jas\min}{time\ taken\ by\ brother} = \frac{r^2}{r^2 - c^2} > 1.$$ Jasmine takes more time than her brother.

23..Let the total number of cartridges of C is 'x' then $x - (4 \times 3) = \frac{1}{3}x$, solving x = 18.

24. Form an equation assuming 'x' as the number of fruits each boy had at the end. The girl collected 45 fruits and distributed to the boys as 8, 5, 12 and 20.

25. Let us assume that the sisters had originally x, y and z apples, x being for the eldest one. After performing the operations as stated in the problem we get the following equations
16x + 4y + 5z = 256
16x + 36y + 13z = 512
16x + 20y + 41z = 512, solving these equations simultaneously we get x = 13, y = 7, z = 4 and the number of apples originally had will be the same as their ages. These are their ages 3 years before. Now their ages will be 16, 10 and 7 years.

26 A gets first because he runs for half the time and naturally the running speed is greater than walking.

27. In 7 hours interval wall clock loses 700 seconds and it will show hrs 6 – 48min. – 20 secs. In one hour

Table clock $3500 \times \frac{37}{36} = 3597$ i.e. loses 3 secs. per hour

Alarm clock $3597 \times \frac{35}{36} = 3497$ i.e. loses 103 secs. per hr.

Wristwatch $3497 \times \dfrac{37}{36} = 3594$ i.e. loses 6 secs. per hour.

The following will be the time shown by the different timepieces at 7 AM news from BBC

Wall clock: Hrs.6 – 48 min.- 20 secs.

Table clock: Hrs.6 – 59 min.- 39 secs.

Alarm clock: Hrs. 6 – 47 min. – 59 secs.

Wrist watch: Hrs. 6 – 59 min. - 18 secs.

28. Assume the speed of slow car as x km/h. Check whether you get the equation $x^2 + 20x – 12,000 = 0$. Solve this to get 100 and 120 km/h.

29. Assume the speed of George as x km/h and try to get the equation $x^2 + 14x – 480 = 0$. George speed is 16 km/h and Tom's speed is 6 km/h.

30. On first meeting the two boats have travelled a combined distance equal to one length of the lake and at the second meeting the combined distance is three lengths of the lake. Elapsed time and distance at second meeting is 3 times as great. The length of lake is $(3 \times 700) – 500 = 1600$m. Since they travel at constant speed $\dfrac{speed\ of\ M}{speed\ of\ N} = \dfrac{700}{1600 – 700} = \dfrac{7}{9}$

31. The will amount written by the lady was £ 8,000. The two sons were having initial saving of £8,000 and £4,000 respectively.

32. Assume original salary as x pounds and form two equations and solve them by equating. £ 600/- per week.

33. Since $216 = 8 \times 27 = 9 \times 24$ she bought 8 kg of sugar at the rate of 27p per kg.

34. Since $a^3 + b^3 = (a + b) (a^2 – ab + b^2)$,
$1,000,027 = 100^3 + 3^3 = (103) (10000 – 300 + 9)$
$= 103 \times 9709 = 103 \times 7 \times 73 \times 19$

35. Let the speed of train is N km per hour and it is x metres long. Form suitable equations and solve. The speed of train is 54 km/h. and it is 450 metres long.

36. Add the second and third equations and substitute the value from first equation.

x+ y + k (x + y) = 10 and k = 4.

37. Assume the distance as D km. Form the equations and solve for D which is 60 km. Assume the required speed to reach at 12 noon as S and form the equations and solve for S which is 12kmph.

38. In one hour Max will type half the report and Julie one third report. Jointly they can do 5/6 portion of the report in an hour. For full report they will together take 1.2 hours or 1hour and 12 minutes.

39. Eighteen years.

40. Let x gm be the weight of syrup and x gm the weight of water taken. At the end the cup A has

$$x - 20 + \frac{2}{3}(x + 20) = \frac{5x - 20}{3} gm$$ The Cup B has $\frac{1}{3}(x + 20)gm$. Equating {cup A}

= 4 {cup B} we solve x = 100. Initially mummy had taken 100gm of syrup and 100gm of water.

41. Suppose I had taken x number of one pound coins and y number of 20p coins. Total I took 100x + 20y pence. When I returned back I had 100y + 20x pence that being one third of the amount I took to the market.
3(100y + 20x) = 100x + 20y, solving we get x = 7y. If we take y = 2, then x = 14 i.e. £14-40p which is approximately £15 as stated in the problem. Therefore, I spent £9-60p in the supermarket.

42. Sum of the roots = 32 and product of roots = 240. Therefore $x^2 - 32x + 240 = 0$, X = 20 or 12. Rita's original pocket money is £20 and that of Ramesh is £12. The inverse ratio is 3 : 5. On the eve of Christmas Rita got £29 and Ramesh got £27.

43. We know that if x, y, z are the roots of a cubical polynomial equation then $a^3 - (x + y + z)a^2 + (xy + yz + zx)a - xyz = 0$ where the roots of a = x, y, or z. According to this formula,
$a^3 - 21a^2 + 146a - 336 = 0$. We can solve this by using remainder theorem. Since the girls are in primary class roots must be within 4 to 10. A = 6, 7 or 8. Hence Mary is 6 years, Seetha is 7 years and Fathima is 8 years old.

44. (x/3) (x/7) = 4x
$x^2 / 21 = 4x$; hence $x^2 - 84x = 0$

x (x – 84) = 0 and x = 0 or 84. If she gets 0 she would not have been happy and hence her distinction mark is 84. Do you feel that her father could find her marks?

45   Let her age when the son was born be x and her father's age was 2.5x. After certain years say 'a' her age was x + a, father's age = 2.5x + a, and son's age = a. But it is given that a = 0.5x Total of all ages = 3.5x + 3a = 5 x = 100 and hence x = 20 years.

46. Number of six-stringed guitars are 43.

47. The younger one is one year and three months and elder sister is six years and three months old.

48. By careful inspection of first and fourth equations we can easily find the solution as 1, 2, 3, 4 and can be further confirmed by substituting in the second and third equations. The inequalities show that Sheela is first, Rahimis second, Ram is third and Shalini is the fourth rank holders.

49. Let the total distance = d km. If father had ridden y km then he had left (x – y). If he had ridden 4y km then he had left. (x – 4y) = ¾ (x –y). This gives y = x/13.
 In case of daughter, if she had travelled z km she had left with (x – z) km If she had travelled z/3, she is left with
X – z/3 = 3(x – z) which gives z = ¾ of x. This shows that father was slower than daughter and hence daughter drove motor-cycle and father rode on the horse back.

1.   Their ages can be anything but must be the same. The two daughters have to be twins!

51. Interchanging of x for u and y for v in equations 1 and 2 produces equations 4 and 3 respectively except for signs of 12 on the right side. Hence substitute u = -x and v = -y in equations I and 2. We will get
  -x + y = 6 and 5x – 3y = -12. Solving these two simultaneously we get x = 3, y = 9, u = -3 and v= -9.

52. This problem is similar to 28. Eight children attended the party.

3

Amusing Nine

This chapter presents some of the peculiarities of '9'

1. Amusing number trick to show to your friends.
Write down the numbers 12345679. Note that the number 8 is omitted. Ask your friend to select any digit. Say 4 is selected, ask him to multiply it by 9 i.e. he gets 36. Ask him to multiply 12345679 by 36 using a calculator
12345679 x 36 = 444444444
You can try by choosing some other digits instead of 4

2. Numbers summing up to 9.
Ask your friend to write any digit numbers. The numbers can be repeated if necessary, but the only condition is that sum of all digits must become 9. For example if she writes 10233 check whether the sum of digits 1+ 0 +2 + 3 + 3 = 9, it is ok. Then ask her to divide 10233 by 9 and there will not be any reminder! Try with some other numbers whose sum of all digits must be always 9.

3. Trick with a three digit number.
Ask your friend to write a three-digit number without showing to you. Then ask her to write it in the reverse order either below or above it and let her subtract. Ask her to tell you any one number in the result leaving the middle. You can tell her the other end number!
Suppose she writes 648, then 846 – 648 = 198. Note that always the middle number will be 9. If she tells 8 then subtract mentally 8 from 9 and tell immediately the other number is 1.

4. A great magical drill on addition.

You are going to perform a lightning-fast calculator work. Ask someone to write a five figure number on the blackboard or on a piece of paper. Suppose he writes 45623, then you leave four places below it to write future numbers which you and some one else may be entering. But to everybody's surprise you can write the total of all the numbers in the beginning itself before they are written. Draw a line at the bottom and subtract always 2 from the digit of the unit place and copy the remaining numbers without forgetting to write 2 at the sixth digit place. So the total will be 245,621.

Below his first number 45623 ask somebody to write the second five figure number. Suppose she writes 67254 write very quickly your choice as 32745 by taking away each of the second row numbers from 9. This must be done mentally without thinking as if you are writing at random. Tell the person to write the fourth five digit number below yours.

Do the same operation and write your 5th row number by taking away each digit from 9. Ask him to sum them all by using a calculator or mentally and it will be a wonder that the total is correct which you wrote in the beginning itself! It is how it works out. The steps are shown below.

		4	5	6	2	3	His choice. (a)
		6	7	2	5	4	Her choice (b)
		3	2	7	4	5	Your choice (c)
		9	0	8	5	8	Someone else choice (d)
			9	1	4	1	Your choice (e)
	2	4	5	6	2	1	Total which you wrote after (a)

5. This is another example similar to 4.

The total is written after your friend completes the fifth row. Just subtract 2 from 4 in row (e) with 701 repeated and write 2 in the 6th digit place.

		6	4	3	8	0	Friend's choice (a)
		3	5	6	1	9	Your choice (b)
		2	7	0	4	3	Friend's choice (c)
		7	2	9	5	6	Your choice (d)
			7	0	1	4	Friend's choice (e)
	2	0	7	0	1	2	Total you wrote after (e)

Note: Tricks 4 & 5 can be done with any number of digits and not necessarily 5 digits as shown in the above examples.

6. Wonderful 1089.

Before you start this game write in a paper the number 1089, put it in an envelope and seal and keep on a table. Ask your friend to write in another piece of paper any three-digit number in which the *first and last digits differ by at least 2*. Tell him to reverse the digits and ask him to find the difference. Suppose first he writes 843 then 843 – 348 = 495. Now ask him to reverse this result and to add i.e. 594 + 495 = 1089. Ask him to keep this as a secret and not to tell you. Then ask him to open the envelope and check whether he finds the same number as he got as the final result. Note the sum of all numbers in this curious 1089 is equal to 9. 1+0+8+9=18 = 1+8 = 9.

7. Some more quick additions game.

I can tell you quickly in less than 9 second that the sum of following six-digit numbers as 4,000,000. How? After understanding the steps you can try for yourself similar instant additions?

671,355---1
508,779---2
183,696---3
882,414---4
328,645---5
491,221---6
816,304---7
117.586---8

How it works?
The first and the fifth lines add up to 1,000,000. Similarly the 2nd and 6th lines add to 1,000,000. Therefore the sum of all numbers will be
4 x 1,000,000 = 4,000,000.

8. Something to do with nine.

Ask a friend to write 4 rows of four digit-numbers one below the other". Then you write 4 rows of four-digit numbers of your choice. To his surprise you can tell the sum of all the 8 rows. But don't show this trick more than once because the answer, 39,996 will be the same.

4,518
2,794
3,057
7,621 all four rows are his numbers.
5,481
7,205
6,942
2,378 above four rows are your numbers

9. The Digit that you crossed out

Write down without showing, a three or more digit number. Divide it by nine and tell me the remainder. Then cross out any number except zero in the originally written number and once again divide by nine. Tell me the remainder, I will tell what number you have crossed out!

10. The number which you crossed out!

Write down any long number of any digits. Then write below a second row composed of numbers of in the first row and find the difference. Cross out any number from the balance except 'zero' if it occurs and tell the sum of the remaining numbers. I will tell the number which you crossed out!

11. The number your friend crossed out.

Jim wrote a number say, 856703, which I don't know. I asked him to cancel any one except zero. So he gets 85703 if he had cancelled 6. I asked him to subtract the digit sum of original number i.e. $8 + 5 + 6 + 7 + 0 + 3 = 29$ from 85703 and he gets 85674. I told him to add each of these digits and to tell me the sum, which is 30. Remember except this 30 that he told in the end of these operations I don't know anything of previous numbers. Immediately I told him that he had cancelled 6. How?

12. Nine divides without remainder!

Ask your friend to write any number of any digits. Let him add each of them and subtract form the original number. Suppose he writes 785402, then let him add the digits like $7 + 8 + 5 + 4 + 0 + 2 = 26$. Then $785402 - 26 = 785376$ which when divided by our magic 9 gives no remainder. This works for any numbers chosen. Can you prove how it works?

13. '1313' is not really an unlucky number!

Ask your friend to write the number 1313 that any one easily remembers. Ask him to subtract any number from it and to make a five–to- seven digit number with the difference on the left and 100 plus the number subtracted on the right. Now he crosses out any non-zero digit and calls out the resulting number. You can promptly name the crossed out digit! See the following example. Suppose he subtracts 48 from 1,313 i.e. $1313 - 48 = 1,265$ and writes this to the left of $(100 + 48)$ becoming 1,265,148. If he crosses 6 and calls out 125148, the digits sum of 125148 is 21. The immediate next number that in the multiple of 9 is 27 and $27 - 21$ is 6 which he crossed out.

14. Multiplier 99

A number with two identical digits is multiplied by 99. What is the four-digit product if the third digit is 5?

15. Remainder with 9 as the divisor.

Suppose we divide 32,145 by 9, immediately we can tell the remainder. Add each digit, 3 + 2 + 1 + 4 + 5 = 15. Again add the digits of 15, 1 + 5 = 6. Hence 6 is the remainder. This method may help to check the division with 9. One more example: When 7,896,432 is divided by 9 the remainder will be 7 + 8 + 9 + 6 + 4 + 3 + 2 = 39. Adding again 3 + 9 = 12 and adding again 1 + 2 = 3. Hence 3 is the remainder. We can use this method as a short-cut to do the problem 9.

Answers: Amusing Nine.

8. Subtract each digit of your friend's numbers from 'nine' and write below the four rows of his numbers. The total will remain the same, 39,996.

9. If he writes 58722 and divides by nine the quotient is 6524 and remainder is 6. Suppose he crosses out 7 in 58722 then 5822 is divided by 9that will give a remainder 8. The crossed number is, 9 – second remainder + first remainder i.e. $9 - 8 + 6 = 7$

10.   This is how it works. Suppose you choose 42,389,107. The second row must contain all these numbers and must be 8 digits same as the first row. Let us say 90,718,342 is chosen then the difference of these two will be
90,718,342 – 42,389,107 = 48329235. Suppose you cross out 8 then sum up the remaining numbers
$4 + 9 + 3 + 2 + 2 + 3 + 5 = 28$. The next higher multiple of 9 is 36 and $36 - 28 = 8$ that is the one you have crossed out.
Suppose you cross out 9 then sum of remaining numbers leaving nine will be 27 which is exactly a multiple of 9 and hence you crossed out 9.

11. Finally he told 30 and the nearest higher number, which is the multiple of 9, is 36. $36 - 30 = 6$ is the number he has cancelled.

12. Suppose the number he wrote is 'abcde'. The value of the sum of digits will be $(10,000a + 1000b + 100c + 10d + e)$. When you take away from this the total of $(a + b + c + e)$ it will be $9,999a + 999b + 99c + 9d$ and no doubt that this is exactly divisible by 9 without remainder.

14. Since 11 is a factor of any two identical-digit number, multiply 99 with 11 and you get 1089. Now check mentally what single digit will multiply 1089 so that the 10 place becomes 5. It is 4. Because $99 \times 44 = 4,356$.

4

Alphabetic Arithmetic

In this chapter we deal with large number of addition and division sums with letters substituted for numbers. This is called as 'cryptarithm' used for coded operations. Identical letters stand for same digits and different letters stand for different digits. An asterisk or any other symbol stands for any digit.

1. Addition sum with letters for numerals (1)
Can you find out and rewrite the problem numerically.

A B C
+
A B C
_____

B B A
_____

2. Addition sum same as above (2)
M A T
+
M M T = A M M

3. Addition of three rows (3)
```
    A B C
+   B B C
    C B C
------------
    D E D
```

4. Addition sum with letters replacing numbers (4).

The same letter stands for the same digit wherever it appears and different letters stand for different digits. Find the numeric values of each letter.

```
  A B C B
+ C D D E
---------------
  A A A B
```

5. Mr. Prickly's pin code number of his credit card.

Here is the total of the following alphabetic sum. Is it possible to find the code number?

```
  Q X X Y
+ A P X X
_____
  P M Y P Q
_____
```

6. Mrs. Pegotty's bank balance.

She wrote in the form of the total of the following alphabetic numbers. What is her bank balance? Any two different letters can't have same values.

```
  R A A P
+ G G A P
_____
  P M B M R
_____
```

7. Messrs. Duncons contractors & Co.

They agreed to take up the job of a bridge construction for a value of the sum given by the following alphabetic addition. The same letter stands for the same digit and different letters stand different digits. Find the tender sum.

```
  Z B C B F X U Q
+
  Z B X I Q U U I
-------------------------
  K Q L Q K F Z B I
```

8. Addition sum with letters replacing numbers. (5)
In the following problem digits have been replaced by alphabets. The same letter stands for the same digit and different letters stand for different digits. Find the total in numerical form.

```
  E B S N N N
+ Q I N Q N N
+ S N H N N N
―――――――――
  G K L B E E
―――――――――
```

9. Alphabetic division replacing numbers.
In the following division each alphabet stands for different digit. Find quotient and remainder.

```
        e z
      ―――――
e s ) s s n      .... (a)
      e s        .... (b)
    ―――――
      e q n      .... (c )
      e q n
    ―――――
```

10. Solve this multiplication: A B C
```
              ×  B A C
          ―――――――――
              *  *  *  *
              *  *  A
        *  *  *  B
        ―――――――――
        *  *  *  *  *  *
```

11. Can you find the value of MOLE
```
              M O L E
          ×   M O L E
        ―――――――――
              *  *  *  *  *
            *  *  *  *  *
          *  *  *  *  *
        *  *  *  *  *
        ―――――――――
        *  *  *  * M O L E
```

57

12. Codeword MORE DAFILOS.

Find the code word from the following equations. You may find two solutions.

M O + R E = D A

F I + L A = S I

R E + L A + S I = L O S

13. Alphabetic division.

In the following division each letter uniquely defines different numbers. Find the exact division.

$$\frac{A\,H\,H\,A\,A\,H}{J\,O\,K\,E} = H\,A$$

14. Alphabetic division.

In the following funny division the only known number is '8' and all the rest are unknowns. Solve it.

```
                  x x 8 x x
        xxx)  x x x x x x x x
                  x x x
                  x x x x
                    x x x
                    x x x x
                    x x x x
```

15. Clover values of the digits.

In the following multiplication more than half of the digits are unknown and marked as ♣. Can you complete the multiplication properly?

```
          ♣ 1 ♣        line 1
        × 3 ♣ 2           2
    ------------------
          ♣ 3 ♣           3
        3 ♣ 2 ♣           4
      ♣ 2 ♣ 5             5
    --------------------
      1 ♣ 8 ♣ 3 0         6
```

FUN WITH MATHS   *ALPHABETIC ARITHMETIC*

16.   Division with missing numbers.

```
3 2 5 ) ☺ 2 ☺ 5 ☺ ( 1 ☺ ☺
        ☺ ☺ ☺
        ----------------
        ☺ 0 ☺ ☺
        ☺ 9 ☺ ☺
        ----------------
          ☺ 5 ☺
          ☺ 5 ☺
          ----------------
```

17.   Multiplication with missing numbers.

```
          ☼ ☼ 5
    ×   1 ☼ ☼
    ----------------
        2☼ ☼ 5
      1 3 ☼ 0
    ☼ ☼ ☼
    ----------------
    4☼ 7 7 ☼
```

18. Only '4' is known in the following division.

```
☼ ☼ ☼ ) ☼ ☼ ☼ ☼ ☼ ☼ ( ☼ 4 ☼ ☼
          ☼ ☼ ☼
        --------------
          ☼ ☼ 4 ☼
          ☼ ☼ ☼ ☼
        ----------------
          ☼ ☼ ☼ ☼
            ☼ 4 ☼
        ----------------
          ☼ ☼ ☼ ☼
          ☼ ☼ ☼ ☼
```

19. Only '7' is known in the following division.

☼ ☼ ☼ ☼ 7 ☼) ☼ ☼ 7 ☼ ☼ ☼ ☼ ☼ ☼ ☼ (☼☼ 7 ☼ ☼
          ☼ ☼ ☼ ☼ ☼

       ☼ ☼ ☼ ☼ ☼ 7 ☼
       ☼ ☼ ☼ ☼ ☼ ☼ ☼

          ☼ 7 ☼ ☼ ☼ ☼
          ☼ 7 ☼ ☼ ☼ ☼

          ☼ ☼ ☼ ☼ ☼ ☼ ☼
          ☼ ☼ ☼ ☼ 7 ☼ ☼

              ☼ ☼ ☼ ☼ ☼ ☼
              ☼ ☼ ☼ ☼ ☼ ☼
              ----

20. Division with wrong numbers.

Mr. Wright entered wrong numbers and made a division problem. But, of course the pattern is right and all the numbers are one out, i.e. either one up or one low. Can you find the correct numbers?

```
9 4 ) 3 9 7 9 ( 8 3        .... (a)
      4 3 9                .... (b)
      ---------
        5 9 9              .... (d)
        7 9 9              .... (e)
      ---------
```

21. Addition with wrong numbers.

Mr Wright once again made a 'carefully careless' problem on addition. All the digits numbers are wrong except that each of them is as usual one out. i.e one more or one less. Find the correct values of the problem.

```
    2 4 7 7 5 7
+     8 0 1 4 5
  -------------------
    1 3 9 2 3 5
  -------------------
```

22. Mr. Wright makes a careful blunder in subtraction.

Mr. Wright is not right in subtraction. All the numbers as usual differ by unity either more or less. But the number digits in each row and pattern are OK. Solve it.

```
      3 0 7 7 5 8
  -    9 1 2 4 5
  -----------------
      2 4 5 3 8 0
  -----------------
```

23. Mr. Wright divides wrongly.

Mr. Wright this time also purposely made a mistake in the process of division. All the digits are wrong and differ by one either up or down. But the number of digits in each row and the pattern of presentation are correct. Solve the problem.

```
    1 5 ) 8 0 1 ( 4 6
          6 9
          --------
          2 4 1
          2 4 1
          ----------
```

24. Hot Mix

In the following 'Hot Mix' problem each alphabet represents a distinct numerical digit. Identify them.

$$7 (H O T, M I X) = 6 (M I X, H O T)$$

25. Star value problem 1.

Find the star values in the following problem.

```
              * 1 *
        ×   3 * 2
        -----------
            * 3 *
        3 * 2 *
      * 2 * 5
      -----------
      1 * 8 * 3 0
      -----------
```

26. Star value problem 2

Solve the following multiplication by determining the values of star as explained in problem 1.

```
        * * 5
   ×  1 * *
   _____
        2 * * 5
    1  3 * 0
    *    * *
   _____
    4  * 7 7 *
```

27. Uncle Jingle bungles

"Uncle Jingle scrambles it wrong
But grumbles a sigh of song,
Find, as you'll appreciate
Mind him to associate
Four or eight or two or six? "

Find which is wrong and values of the stars and give a friendly hand to Uncle Jingle.

```
         2 *
  4 * ) * * * 8
       * * *
      _____
         * *
       6 *
      _____
```

28. Star multiplication without numbers.

In this remarkable cryptarithm each digit is a prime number less than 10. Solve the problem completely.

```
        * * *
         * *
      _____
       * * * *
      * * * *
      _____
      * * * * *
```

29. Annual bonus.

Annual bonus amount of £ ☺ ☺ is distributed to a number ☺ ☺ ☺ of workers in a clothing factory. How much of total amount was distributed. In every step of long multiplication each single digit number is a prime number.

```
        ☺ ☺ ☺
    ×     ☺ ☺
    ------------------
      ☺ ☺ ☺ ☺
    ☺ ☺ ☺ ☺
    ------------------
    ☺ ☺ ☺ ☺ ☺
```

30. Real estate owner.

A real estate owner spills coffee on his document in which all numbers except 0, 7, and 3 were erased and the calculations appeared as shown below. Can you get back the missing numbers?

```
              ☺ ☺ ☺ ☺
  ☺ ☺ ) ☺ ☺ ☺ ☺ 0 ☺          .... (a)
         ☺ ☺                  .... (b)
       ----------------------
            ☺ ☺ ☺             .... (c)
            ☺ ☺ 7             .... (d)
       ----------------------
               ☺ ☺            .... (e)
               3 ☺            .... (f)
       ----------------------
```

31. Cryptic multiplication.

Schwetha made an ordinary multiplication and to make it as a puzzle she replaced every even digits with E and odd digits with letter O. She obtained the steps as shown below. What exactly was her multiplication?

```
        E O E
    ×     O O
    ------------
      O O O E
    O O O E
    ------------------
      O E E O E
    ------------------
```

32. Dog square.

One day the smart David was scribbling some thing in his note book during history lesson. The teacher grabbed the note book and found the following statement.

$(DOG)^2 = DDAAB$

The teacher asked him to explain this non-sensual statement on the board. He wrote as shown below.

```
        D O G
    ×   D O G
-------------------
          G A B
    D O G
-------------------
    D D A A B
-------------------
```

David gave clue that G is a prime number and B is an odd number and also square of an odd number. So what is the value of "Dog square"?

Bertrand Russell (1872 – 1970). He tried to reduce all mathematics knowledge into formal logic. He is the pioneer to set, vectors and functions. He showed that the idea of a set of all sets which are not members of themselves leads to contradictions. His ideas of controversy got him dismissed from Trinity College, Cambridge and also from City College, New York. He made himself prominent public figure and died at the age of 97.

Answers: Alphabetic Arithmetic

1. A = 4, B = 9 and C = 7. Remember that in the addition of each column not more than 1 can be carried out. From the addition of units column we have 1 carried over so that 1 + B + B = 19. The addition of 100$_s$ column is 1 + A + A = B. This is possible only when B = 9 and A = 4. Hence C = 7

2.. M = 4; A = 9; T = 7

3. A+B+C = D. A single digit and no 1. Therefore A, B and C are different and their sum 2+3+4 = 9. D = 9; 3C = 9, C = 3, B = 2, A = 4. 423 + 223 + 323 = 969

4   A = 1, B = 8, C =9, D = 2. E = 0. The most that can be carried over on addition is 1. Hence all the A$_s$ are 1. B + E = B, this shows that E must be 0 and there is nothing to carry in this sum. In 1000$_s$ column 1 + A + C = A. Since we already found that A = 1, C must be 9. From 10$_s$ column 9 + D = 1 that means D must be equal to 2. From 100$_s$ column 1 + B + 2 = 1 which shows that B= 8.

5. Q = 2, X = 5, Y = 7, A = 8, P = 1, M = 0.

6. As usual P = 1 and hence R = 2. This leaves that M is not equal to 1 or 2 because two letters can not have the same value. 1 + 2 + G = M, and G can't be 8 or 9. G can't be 6 or less than 6 since 3 + G must be equal to a two digit number. Hence G = 7 and M = 0. A – 5. This shows that Mrs. Pegolly's bank balance is £10,302.

7.   Since Q + I = I the value of Q = 0 and K = 1. 2Z = 10 and Z = 5. Since Q = 0 the first two columns do not have carry over. X + U = 5, X or U can't be 1 but either of them 2 or 3. C is not equal to 0, 1, 2, 3 and 4 and U = 2, X = 3. Third and fourth columns also do not have carry over. B + I = K = 1, B = 4 and hence I = 7. Since B + I has carry over. 1 + C + 3 = 0, C is 6 and L = 9. Since all numeric values have been assigned except 8, F must be 8. Hence the tendered value is £109,018,547.

8.   1st column addition is not having carry over and the 5th and 6th columns do not have carry over. N must be 3 or less than 3. If N = 3 then E will be 9 making a carry over for the 6th column. If N = 2 then E = 6 and with 3 in the 1st column Q and S can't be 2 because already we took N=2. If we take Q=1 and S=3 then total is 10 which is also not possible. Therefore N = 1 and E = 3. Q and S must be 4 and 2 or 2 and 4. Therefore G = 9. If Q is taken to be 2 in the 4th

column B = 4. This is not allowed since we assigned 4 for Q or S. Therefore Q = 4, S = 2 and B = 6. 2nd column has nothing to carry. 7 + I = K. By little reasoning K = 7 and I = 0. The 3rd column 3 + H= L and L = 8 and H = 5.
Hence the total is 978,633.

9.. Remainder is zero. Before you start solving draw the above problem with letters replaced by dashes (-) and as you find the numbers write them in respective places. Since (b) is the same as divisor e must be 1. s take away s must be zero and hence q = 0. s – e = e. i.e. s – 1 = 1, s = 2. The divisor is 12. 22 – 12 = 10. Hence q = 0. 12 x 9 = 108. Therefore n = 8 and z = 9. The quotient is 19 and remainder is 0.

10. 286 x 826 = 236,236

11. MOLE = 9,376.

12.   From eq. 2, A = 0, O + E = 10
MORE DAFILOS = 34569072148 or 23679048135

13. We can write the given division as AHHAAH ÷ HA = JOKE = $100 + \dfrac{AH(10{,}001)}{HA}$. But the factors of 10.001 is 73 x 137. Hence the given problem is 377,337 / 73 = 5169.

14. Note that 8 times divisor < 1000, so divisor < 125. 7 times divisor < 900 and hence from the first subtraction that the first digit of the quotient is 8 and it further follows that the quotient is 80,809. Since 80809 times divisor < 10,000,000 we get divisor >123 and hence divisor is 124 and 124 x 80809 = 10,020,316.

15.   415 x 382 = 158530. Since the answer for the product ends with 0, the unit place in line 3 must be 0. The unit place for line 1 has to be either 0 or 5. The tens place of line 3 is 3. Hence the unit place of line can not be 0 and it must be 5. The tens place of answer is 3 which reasons out that the unit digit of line 4 is 0. Tens place of line 2 must be 8 because 8 times 15 from line 1 gives 120. The 100_s place in line 1 must be 4 because 4 times 8 make 32 i.e. the number 3 is the starting one in line 4. Hence the problem solved.

16.   52,650 ÷ 325 = 162.

17.   325 x 147 = 47,775

18.   There are more than one solution for this problem.
a. $1,337,174 \div 943 = 1,418$
b. $1,343,784 \div 949 = 1,416$
c. $1,200,474 \div 846 = 1,419$
d. $1,202,464 \div 848 = 1,418$

19.   There is only one solution for this.
       $7,375,428,413 \div 125,473 = 58,781$.   These two problems, 18 and 19 are slightly difficult to solve. They are challenging tasks for the attempters. They first appeared in the American publications 'School World, 1906 and Mathematical Magazine, 1920'.

20.   Remainder is zero. Mark each line as a, b, c, d for convenience. The first two numbers of dividend must be either 28 or 40. Divisor must be 85 or 83. First number of quotient must be 2 or 4. Since $2 \times 85 = 170$, number 2 is ruled out and it must be 4. So the quotient is 48.
       $4 \times 83 = 332$ and $4 \times 85 = 340$. . The trial shows that dividend is 4080.. Hence the problem is $4080 \div 85 = 48$.

21.   The correct answer is given below. Try for yourselves.

```
     156868
  +   91256
  ------------------
     248124
  ------------------
```

22.   The correct answer is given below. Try for yourselves.

```
     418647
  -   82356
  ------------------
     336291
  ------------------
```

23. $910 \div 26 = 35$. Method of working is not shown.

24. Let HOT = x and MIX = y, then
       $7\{1000 \text{ (HOT)} + \text{MIX}\} = 6\{1000 \text{ (MIX)} + \text{HOT}\}$
       $7000x + 7y = 6000y + 6x$

6,994x = 5,993y, dividing by 13
538x = 461y, Therefore, HOT MIX = 461,538

25. Since the result shows 0 in the unit place, the first digit in the third line is 0. Since 2 x 5 = 10, the first digit in line 1 is 5. From line 5, value of 3 x 4 = * 2 = 12. Therefore first line is 415 and third line is 830. Fifth line is 1245. Fourth line is 3320. Sixth line is 158530. Dividing the fourth line, 3320 by first line, 415 we get 8 and hence the second line is 382. This completes the problem.

26. Line 1 is 325. Line 2 is 147. Line 3 is 2275. Line 4 is 1300. Line 5 is 325. Last line is 47775.

27. Line 1 = 28. Line 2 = 68)1428 . Line 3 = 136.
Line 4 = 68. Line 5 = 68. Remainder = 0.

28. Answer: 775 X 33 = 25,575

29. Single digit prime numbers are 2, 3, 5, 7. The possibilities for the first row of multiplication to have primes: 3 x 775 = 2325 or 5 x 555 = 2775 or 5 x 755 = 3775 or 7 x 325 = 2275. Hence the multiplication works out to

```
        775
   ×     33
   -----------
      2325
      2325
   ----------
     25575
```

30. Remainder is zero. Row e = 3☺. The divisor is 3☺. The unit digit of quotient is 1. The row c is ☺00. Row d must be 297 and the divisor must be 33.and the quotient is now ☺☺91. Row c is 300 making the dividend ☺☺☺003. Since two zeroes are brought down in row the quotient is now ☺091. The first digit of quotient can't be 2 and less or 4 and above and must be 3. Hence the problem is 102003 ÷ 33 = 3091.

31. 438 × 33 = 14454. Check whether there will be any other possible solutions available.

32. $107^2 = 11449$

Gauss, Karl Friedrich. Born in 1777. German mathematician and astronomer. Patronized by the Duke of Brunswick, who defrayed the expenses of his education at Brunswick and Gottingen, where in 1801 Gauss produced "Disquisitiones Arithmeticae." In 1807 Gauss became professor and director of the observatory at Gottingen, and held the position until his death in 1855. During this period, he brought out many works on pure mathematics, astronomy, and other sciences, among which the chief are "Theoria Motus Corporum Coelestium, in Sectionibus Conicis Ambientium."

5.

DIVISIBILITY

Even numbers can not divide an odd number without a reminder. But an odd number can divide an even or odd number unless the dividend is a prime number.

1.   Famous '2,520'.
Archaeologists discovered in hieroglyphs the number '2,520' engraved on the stone lid of a tomb in an Egyptian pyramid. Why was such an honour paid for this number?

2.   Divisibility by '2'.
2 can divide numbers ending with 0,2,4,6,8

3.   Divisibility by '3'.
Check whether 3 can divide 789. Add all the digits. 7 + 8 + 9 = 24 and this 24 is evenly divisible by 3. Hence 3 can divide 789. For example 3 can not divide 688 since the sum of digits is 22 that can not be divided exactly by 3.

4.   Divisibility by '4'.
Check the last two digits of the given number. If there are two zeros or the two numbers can be divided by 4 then the whole of given number can be divided evenly by 4. 866700 can be divided by 4 because it ends with the last two digits with two zeros.
can also divide 866784 evenly because the last two digits i.e. 84 is divisible by 4.

5.   Divisibility by '5'.
Any number that ends with 5 or 0 is evenly divisible by 5. For example 3,867,255 ÷ 5 = 773,451.

6. Divisibility by '6'

There are two conditions for this.

The number must be even.

The digit sum of the number must be divisible by three.

The number 27,354 ends with 4 which is even and the digit sum is $2 + 7 + 3 + 5 + 4 = 21$ which is divisible by 3 and hence 6 can divide 27,354.

7. Check for divisibility by 3, 7 and 19.

Russians like the number 7. Their folk songs and proverbs use seven very often. Here are few of them.

"Measure cloth seven times before you cut it once.

Seven misfortunes, one reckoning.

One ploughs, seven come along with spoons.

A baby had seven nurses, yet lost his eye."

Let us see whether 138,264 is divisible by 3, 7 and 19. Remove the last two numbers, 64 and multiply it with 4 and add to the remaining numbers. $1382 + 4 \times 64 = 1638$. Repeat the same procedure. $16 + 4 \times 38 = 168$. We can stop here and check mentally whether 168 is divisible by 3, 7 or 19. 168 is divisible by 3 and 7 and not by 19. Hence 138,264 is divisible by 3 and 7 but not by 19.

8. Check for divisibility by 7, 11 and 13.

These are consecutive prime numbers and their LCM is 1,001. Suppose you want to test the divisibility of 42,623,295. Separate the numbers as 42 and 623 and 295. Do the following operation. $623 - (42 + 295) = 286$. Since 286 is divisible by 11 and 13 and not by 7. Hence the same with the given number, 42,623,295.

9. Divisibility by '8'.

The last three digits must be zeros or the 8 must divide the last three digits. For example 579,000 is divisible by 8 and 579,152 is also divisible by 8 since 8 can divide 152.

10. Divisibility by '9'.

Add up all the digits of the number and the sum must be divisible by 9.

Let us consider the number 91,395, The digit sum is 27 which is divisible by 9 and therefore 9 can divide 91,395.

11. Divisibility by '10'.

Obviously any number ending with zero.

12. Divisibility by '11'.

If it is a three-digit number then the sum of the end numbers must be equal to the middle one. Example 231 is divisible by 11 because 2 + 1 = 3, the middle number. If it is a three-digit number with the sum exceeding the middle number by 11 then it is possible.

Example: 979 is divisible by 11 because 9 + 9 = 18 and 18 – 7 = 11.

Even number of digits with same numbers is divisible by 11 For example 777,777 is divisible by 11,

For any type of digits with different numbers follow the method shown. Add the digits that are in the odd slots and add the digits in the even order of slots. Find the difference of these sums and if it results with zero or divisible by 11 then it is possible.

Example:4,957,623. Sum of odd slot numbers 3 + 6 + 5 + 4 = 18 and sum of even slot numbers 2 + 7 + 9 = 18. Then 18 – 18 = 0 and hence 4,957,623 is divisible by 11.

Suppose the number is 304,062. Sum of odd slot numbers 2 + 0 + 0 = 2 and sum of even slot numbers 6 + 4 + 3 = 13. Then the 13 – 2 = 11 which is divisible by 11 and hence it is possible.

13. Divisibility by '12'.

If a number is divisible by 3 and 4 individually then 12 can divide it. Apply the rules stated for divisibility by 3 and 4 individually.

Suppose 508,272 is the number. Apply the check for divisibility by 3. The digit sum is 24, which can be divided by 3. The last two digits, 72 can be divided by 4 and hence the given number is divisible by 12.

14. Divisibility by '15'.

When a numbers happens to be divisible by 3 and also by 5, then it can very well be divided by 15.

15. Divisibility by '20'.

The number should have units digit as '0' and the tens digit is even.

16. Divisibility by '22'.

The number must be even and also must be divisible by 11.

17. Divisibility by '24'.

The number must be simultaneously divisible by 3 and also by 8. Apply the corresponding rules for the divisibility by 3 and 8

18. Divisibility by '25'.
The number must end with '00', multiples of 25.

19. Divisibility by '30'.
The number must end with '0' and divisible by 3

20. Divisibility by '33'.
The number must be divisible individually by 3 and 11.

21. Divisibility by '36'.
The number must be divisible individually by 4 and 9.

Similarly you can form your own rule for the divisibility by other numbers by knowing their basic factors.

22. LCM of 7, 8, and 9.
I am thinking a number of three digits. If you subtract 7 from it, the result is divisible by 7. If 8 is subtracted it is divisible by 8 and if 9 it is divisible by 9. What is the number?

23. Egg seller.
A woman was carrying a basket with eggs and on her way to market she was hit by a cyclist. The basket fell down and all the eggs were broken. To compensate this havoc by paying money the cyclist asked her how many eggs she was carrying.
"I don't remember" the lady who was mathematically shrewd said, "but I do recall that as I divide the eggs by 2, 3, 4, 5 and 6 the remainder is 1. When I heap them in groups of 7, I can empty the basket."
What is the least number of eggs that were broken?

24. Our teacher.
Our teacher once asked each of four children to think of a four-digit number. "Now please transfer the first digit to the end and add the new number to your originally thought one. For example, 1,234 + 2,341 = 3,575. Tell me your results". The children replied as:
Ramu: 8,612. Ashvi: 9,867. Paul: 4,322. Sheela: 13,859
"Every one except Ashvi are wrong," said the teacher. How did the teacher know?

25. Divisibility by 396
Find the probability that if the single digit 0 to 9 is placed at random in place of the symbol ☺ in the following giant number so that the resulting number is divisible by 396.

5 ☺ 383 ☺8☺2☺936☺5☺8☺203☺9☺3☺76

26. Ships at Portsmouth harbour
Four ships leave Portsmouth harbour on Christmas day, Saturday, 25th December 2004. The first ship returns to this port every 4 weeks, the second every 8 weeks, the third every 12 weeks and the fourth every 16 weeks. When did the captains of the four ships meet together in this port?

27. Temperature equation.
$$[3(273 + a)]^2 = 492,b04$$
In the above said equation find the digits symbolised by 'a' and 'b'.

28. Divisibility by 37 helps
When a friend writes a three digit number you can add quickly three or even six more digits so that the resulting six or nine digit number is divisible by 37. Note that the numbers 111, 222, etc. repeating numbers say, 555,555,555,555 in-groups of 3 is divisible by 37. Suppose your friend writes 412 subtract it from say, 777 mentally or secretly and either prefix or affix with 412 likes 365,412 or 412,365. Ask him to check with calculator the successful divisibility with 37.

29. Two theorems on divisibility by 7
Theorem 1:
If a two digit number represented by AB is divisible by 7, then the number BA + A is also divisible by 7. For the number 63 that is divisible by 7, 36 +6 = 42 is also divisible by seven.
Theorem 2 :
 If a three digit number, ABC is divisible by 7, then CBA – (C – A) is also divisible by 7. For the number 602 that is divisible by 7, 206 –(2 – 6) = 210 is also divisible by seven.

30. Sharing between brothers.
 Mr. Patrick wants to distribute £ 316 to his two sons such that each of them gets more than £100 and one part is divisible by 13 while the other part is divisible by 11. Find the amount taken by each of them.

31. Dividing by '9'.
Problem 10 explains the divisibility by 9. A short cut to divide any number by nine is given herewith. Suppose we want to divide 42 by 9, the first digit 4 is the quotient and 4 + 2 = 6 is the remainder.
Find 46 ÷ 9. When we add 4 + 6 = 10, and the division of 10 by 9 gives 1 r 1. Add 1 to 4 and now 5 is the quotient and 1 remainder.

32. Division fantasy:
Let us close this chapter with the following arrangements of four ten digits numbers.
a) 2,438,195,760;   b) 4,876,391,520;
c) 3,785,942,160   and   d) 4,753,869,120
Surprisingly each of the four numbers given above are divisible by
2,3,4,5,6,7,8,9,10,11,12,13,14,15,16,17, and 18.

Leonard Euler (1707 – 1783). Swiss mathematician but moved to Russia and later to Berlin. Euler's works can be summed up by saying that he created a good deal of analysis, and revised almost all the branches of pure mathematics which were then known, filling up the details, adding proofs, and arranging the whole in a consistent form. Such work is very important, and it is fortunate for science when it fall into hands as competent as those of Euler.

Answers: Divisibility

1. Perhaps this is the only smallest number that can be divided by every integers from 1 to 10.

The lowest common multiple, LCM of 7, 8 and 9 that is 504.

23. The LCM of 2, 3, 4, 5, 6 is 60. The total number of eggs must be 60n + 1 and this must be divisible by 7.
60n + 1 = 7x8n + (4n + 1). This shows that 4n + 1 must be divisible by 7. The smallest value of 'n' that can satisfy this condition is 5. Hence 301 eggs!

24. The four digit number 'abcd' can be written as 1000a+100b+10c+d, by transposing a to d we have
1000b+100c+10d+a. Adding these two we get
1001a+1100b+110c+11d. This total is divisible by 11.
Ashvi's answer is 9867 that can be divided by 11.

25. The last two digits, 76 is divisible by 4. Sum of all digits, 45 and hence the given number is divisible by 9. The sum of even placed digits is 73. Sum of numbers 0 to 9 is 45. The sum of odd placed digits, regardless of the order in which the blanks are filled is 62. 73 – 62 = 11 which is divisible by 11. The product (4) (9) (11) = 396. Hence the probability is unity.

26. LCM of 4,8,12 and 16 is 48. So they will meet after 48 weeks i.e. on 19th November 2005.

27. The left-hand side of the equation is divisible by 9 because of the factor 32. The sum of digits on the right side is 19 + b and the closest value of b = 8 for divisibility with 9. Hence a = - 39 and b = 8.

30. Elder son gets £195 and the younger son gets £121.

6

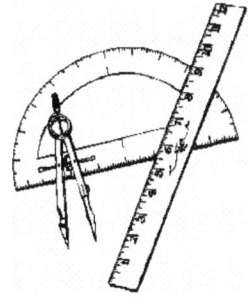

Geometric Gymnastics

1. Properties of polygon

Let us consider a symmetrical two-dimensional pattern, say an octagon. By joining the corners we get the figure as shown below.

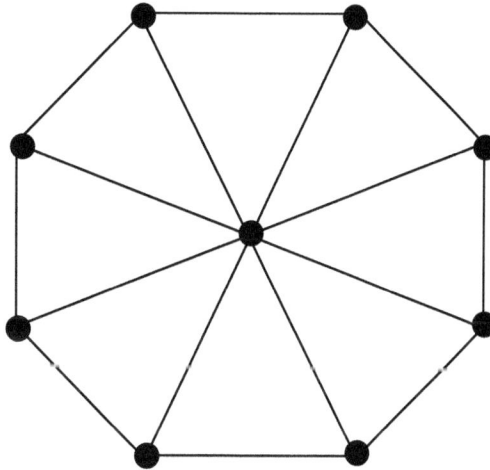

From the figure notice that there are 9 black dots (D), 8 closed spaces (S) and 16 lines (L) connecting the dots. The following equation can be obtained.

D	+	S	-	L	=	1
9	+	8	-	16	=	1

It can be found that this equation always yields to 1 for any geometrical shapes provided only the enclosed shapes are counted. The polygon may be either closed or open type

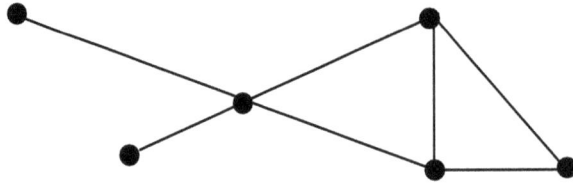

According to the same equation for this open, irregular polygon
D +   S - L = 6 + 2 − 7 = 1
Now try with any other shapes and check!

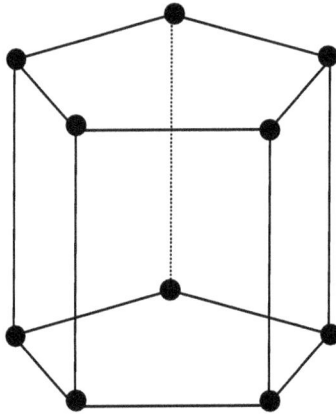

2.   Solids

If the object is a three-dimensional shape like Prisms, Cuboid, Pyramid etc. what happens to that equation? Let us try a case. The above pentagonal prism has 10 dots, 7 spaces and 15 lines. Hence the equation becomes
D + S - L = 10 + 7 - 15 = 2. In case of all three-dimensioned objects the result is always 2. You can try this with an Egyptian Pyramid!

3.   Polygons and internal angle.

AB, BC and CD are three consecutive sides of a regular polygon. If the angle ACD is equal to 144 how many sides are there in this regular polygon?

4.   Angle inside a star

Find the value of the angle E in the figure shown below. Note that it is not necessary that BC is to be parallel with AB.

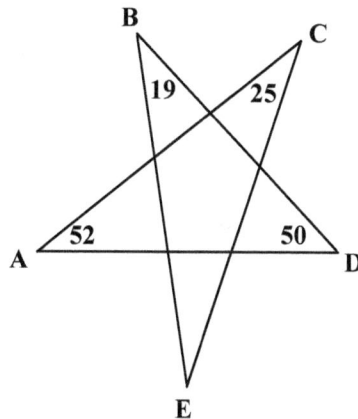

5. **Find the missing number in the following figure**

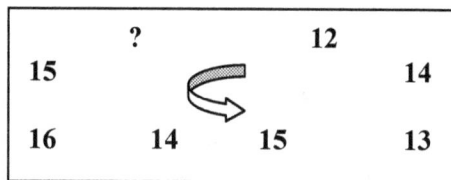

6. **Orthogonal circles**

A circle of radius 15 cm intersects another circle of radius 20 cm orthogonal i.e. at the point of intersection the tangent drawn to one circle is the radius to the other circle.   What is the difference of the areas of the non-overlapping portions?

7.   **Centre of a given circle**

Do you know how to find the centre of a given circle using only a set-square and a pencil? Read the method shown below.

Method: On the circumference of the circle place the set-square such that the corner with 90° and mark the intersecting points A and B where the base of the set-square cuts the circle's circumference.   Similarly keep the top of set-square at some other point on the circle and mark the intersecting points of the base with the circumference as C and D. Join AB and CD.   The intersection of AB and CD is the centre of the circle.

8. Dividing a crescent.

Can you divide a crescent into six parts using only two straight lines? I have shown a method for you to try with your friends.

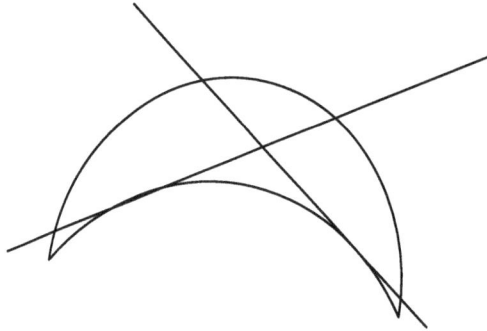

9. Angles magnified

If two lines intersecting at 2° is looked through a lens of magnifying power four times how much bigger the angle will appear?

10. Eiffel tower

The Eiffel tower at Paris is 300 metre tall and is made of 80,000,000 kg of steel. I wish to make a model of this tower with one kg of steel. What will be the height of the model tower? Assume while melting and finishing the metal is not wasted.

11. Octagonal frame.

Cut a copy of the **octagonal frame** into 8 congruent parts and with them form an 8-paired star with the octagonal hole in the centre.

Method is shown below:

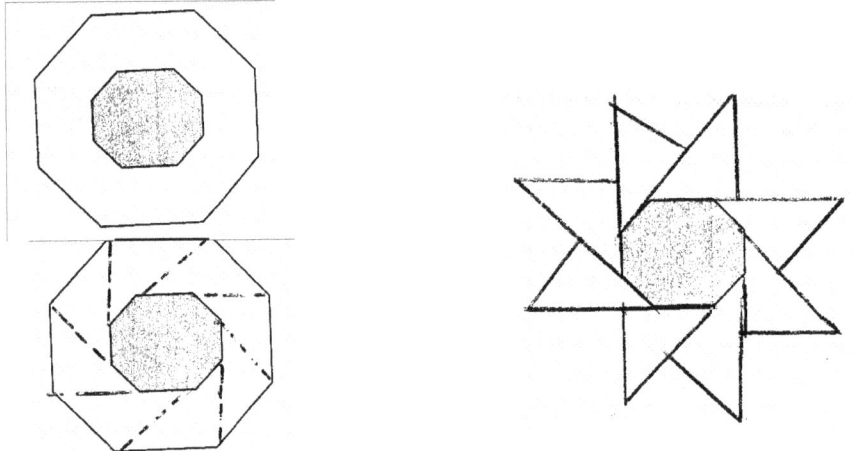

12. Triangle and a regular hexagon

An equilateral triangle and a regular hexagon have equal perimeters. What is the ratio of their areas?

13.   Temple tower.

There is a tall temple tower in my village. I have a photo of this tower. Can you suggest a method to know approximately the real height of the tower?

14. Draught coins

Place three white pieces in squares 1, 2, and 3 of the figure and three black pieces on squares 5, 6, and 7. Shift the white pieces to the squares occupied by the black ones and vice versa. You may move a piece forward in the adjacent unoccupied square.   If any piece needs to jump it can do so by jumping over one of the forward piece. Whole thing must be rearranged in 15 moves.

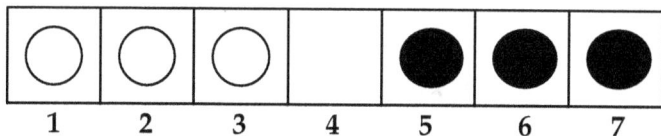

(This is left for the readers to try for themselves)

15. Draw three lines

Draw three lines across the rectangle shown below from alphabet to alphabet so that you get five plots and each area contains three circles.

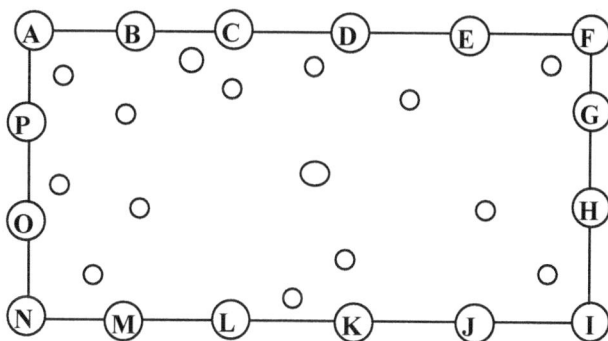

16. Making a pentagon

Using long strip of paper make a single knot as if you are doing with a thread and care fully press by flattening the knot. See the figure below.

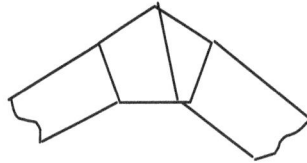

17. Circular discs

The figure below shows 10 numbers of circular discs each of them marked alphabetically. Move only as minimum number of discs as possible, so that it looks the same but the base up and vertex down.

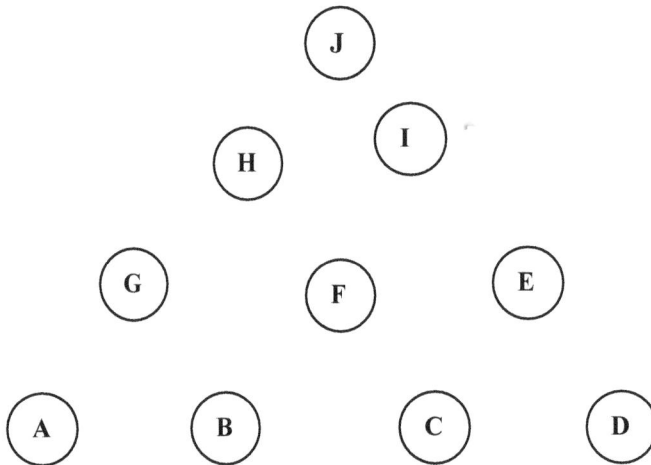

18. A stone block

A stone block is in rectangular shape and it weighs 4 kg. If a toy model, one fourth of its size is made with same material what will be its weight? Assume the specific gravity of stone as 2.4.

19. Watermelons seller.

A man sells two watermelons; one is one and quarter times bigger than the other. The cost of bigger fruit is one and half times the smaller one. Which is profitable to buy?

20. Joycee and her cherry fruits.

Joycee selects a cherry fruit that is almost spherical in shape. She cuts exactly in the middle and finds the thickness of fruit flesh is same as the diameter of the seed. Can you workout mentally how much more the flesh part of the fruit than the seed?

21. Rate of cooling and geometrical shapes.

Water at 99° C is filled in two cups of similar shape and material but one is bigger in size to the other. Water in which cup gets cooler first?

22. Mother and child in winter cold.

A mother and her child in Finland are dressed with same type of woollen clothes and stand in the street. Who will feel colder?

23. Crossing to reach centre platform.

A square shaped pond with water has a square platform in the centre. The pond is 12m x 12m and the platform is 2m x 2m. Peter has two wooden planks of sufficient width and each of 4.8 metres length. Suggest a suitable plan for him to reach the centrally placed platform. Poor fellow, he doesn't know how to swim.

24. Volumes ratio of the truncated cone.

A solid metal cone of height 6 cm is cut into three parts so that the height of each part is 2 cm, the planes of cutting being parallel. Calculate the ratio of the volumes of the three parts.

25. Mary and her pancake.

Mary made a very big pancake of hexagonal shape with each side measuring 12 cm for the party. Unexpectedly there were guest of five adults and six kids.
Mum got worried how Mary is going to cut the pancake because she wanted five equally bigger sizes for the adults and six equally smaller sizes for the children so that there won't be any misunderstanding.
Shrewd Mary solved the problem because she is a geometric gymnastic!
But how she solved this cutting problem?
What area of pan cake each adult and each child will be getting assuming there is no wastage?

26. Tractor wheels

A tractor is having the front two wheels smaller in diameter compared with the two rear wheels. It is found that the front wheels get worn out quicker than the rear wheels. Why?

27. In six lines....

Can you make 24 students to stand in six lines so that in each line there are five of them standing?

28. Crazy triangle.

Can you draw a triangle with 90° at all the three corners?

29. Drill master's puzzle.

The drill master Mr. Fredrick wanted his nine students to stand in ten rows! Is it possible? But he was sure and he made it also! How?

30. Cutting a cube.

Mary wants to cut a cubical shaped cheese in to
a)   An equilateral triangle.
b)   A regular hexagon.

31. Cutting a circle.

Is it possible to cut a circle in to 22 parts with 6 straight lines? The parts need not be equal but may form some symmetrical divisions. You can not do with diameters. Six diameters can make twelve parts only!

Pythagoras (569 – 500 BC). The great Greek mathematician. He settled in southern Italy and formed a mysterious brotherhood with his students who under the oath were prevented to reveal the secrets of numbers. They laid the foundation for arithmetic through geometry. They failed to resolve the concept of irrational numbers. At later stage Euclid of Alexandria was successful and brought out a book.

Answers: Geometric gymnastics.

3.   15 sides.   4). 34°.   5) 17

6. Overlapping area = 166 cm². Difference of non-overlapping areas = 9 cm².

9.   Same.   10).   Height of model tower will be 1.5 m.

12.   The sides of the triangle and hexagon are in the ratio 2 : 1, The area of hexagon is 1.5 times the area of triangle.

13. Measure width and height of the tower in the photo say 5cm and 22cm. Also measure base width of the real tower say it is 6m.   Then ht. of tower = $\dfrac{6x22}{5} = 26.4m$.

15.   One of the solutions: Join B to K, K to E and E to O

17.   J moves clockwise down to next of I on its right side. A moves up to the left side of H. D comes below B and C as the new vertex.

18. 62.5 gms   19. The bigger fruit.

20. Ratio of diameter of seed to that of whole fruit is 1to 3. Volume ratio is 1 to 27. Otherwise the flesh part is 26 times more than seed in volume.

21.   Q = MST, where Q = mass of heat, S = Specific heat of material and T = change in temperature. Smaller cup cools first.

22.   Child. Same reason as stated in (21).

23   Arrange the two planks in the shape of T near any corner of the pond.

24. The volume ratios are 1 : 7 : 19.

25. Mary's plan for cutting the pancake.

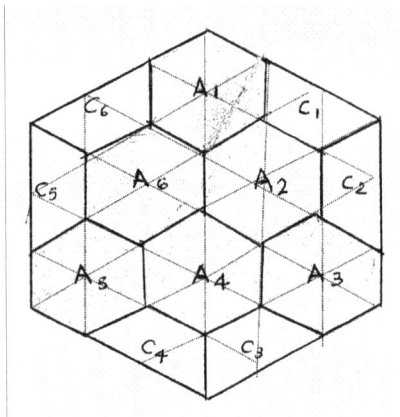

A for adults

C for children

The area of full pan cake is 374.12 cm^2. Area of adult's pan cake is 41.57 cm^2 and child's pan cake is 20.8 cm^2. Note that there are six big pieces. The shrewd Mary purposely cut six pieces and reserved one for herself!

26.   For a particular distance of travel the front wheels rotate more number of times than the rear ones.

27.

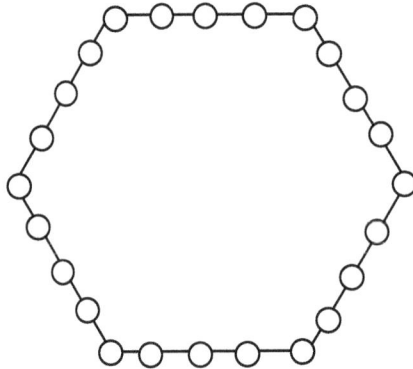

28.   This is possible in a three dimensional plane. Consider a foot ball of perfect sphere. In a hemi-sphere of this ball draw two meridian lines at 90° then the spherical triangle formed with equator as the base is having all the angles as right angle.

29.

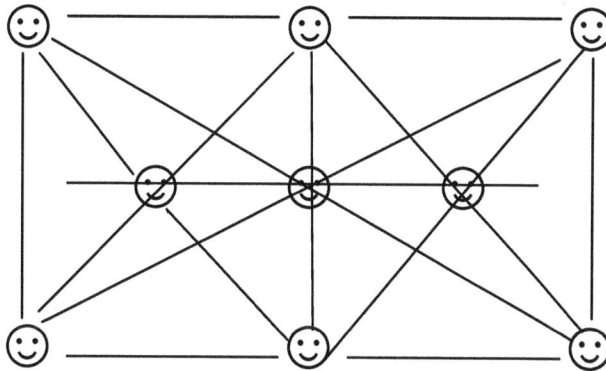

30

30 (a)

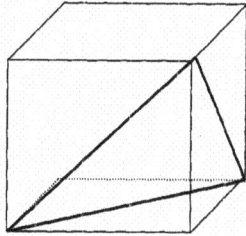

30 (b)

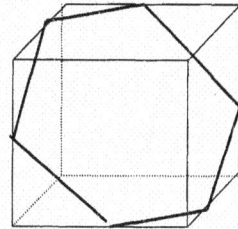

31. To get maximum number of parts every line should intersect all other lines and no more than two lines should intersect at any point. By induction one can get the general formula for the number of parts, $p = \frac{1}{2}(n^2 + n + 2)$ where $n =$ number of straight lines. If $n = 6$ the maximum number of parts $p = 22$

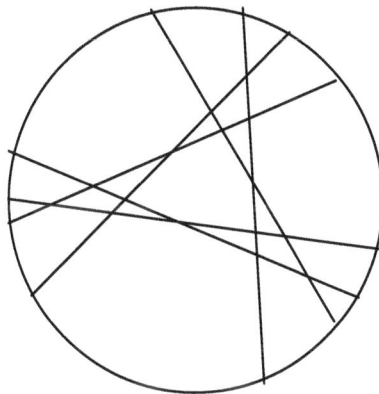

7

GIANT NUMBERS

This chapter presents many entertaining problems of oddities involving with numbers 0 to 9 but extending to infinity!

1.   Rumour spreads at hypersonic speed.

The speed with which rumours spread is really fantastic. Once I told my friend for fun that I got one million pounds in the National Lotto. Within five seconds I got thousands of phone messages and personal visiting. Here is a problem showing mathematically the swiftness of rumour spreading.

Suppose I live in a town with population of 50,000 assuming I told my Lotto winning to three people in my house and I took 15 minutes for this announcement. At 8-15 AM $1 + 3 = 4$ people including me know this. Each of them makes a secret announcement to three individuals in turn. Within 15 minutes i.e. at 8-30 AM the news is known including me to $1 + 3 + (3 \times 3) = 13$ persons. At 8-45 in this way $13 + (3 \times 9) = 40$ knows it.

At 9 AM $40 + (3 \times 27) = 121$ people
At 9-15 AM $121 + (3 \times 81) = 364$ people
At 9-30 AM $364 + (3 \times 3^5) = 1,093$ people

If you work in this way you may find that by 10-30 AM on the same day the whole town of 50,000 are becoming aware that I am a millionaire!

2.   Trick from Hindu legend.

Place three plates A, B and C on a table, B in the middle and put coins of denominations £1 at the bottom followed by 50p, 20p, 10p and at the top 5p in the same order on the plate A. Now the task to be done is to rearrange the coins in the same order on the plate C strictly following the rules given below. Always you have to shift the coin on the top most place.

a)   Only one coin at a time to be moved.

b)   Never place a higher denomination coin over a smaller denomination one.

If you are successful count how many minimum numbers of movements you have made. Do not lose hope. Try and try till you get bored!

Suppose you are to try to do this with only two coins i.e. 10p and 5p the following steps will count for three moves. 5B, 10C and 5C. (5C means 5p coin is moved to plate C).

If it is with three coins i.e. 20p, 10p and 5p the minimum number of moves will be 5C, 10B, 5B, 20C, 5A, 10C and 5C making 7 moves.

If it is with 4 coins i.e. 50p, 20p, 10p and 5p. Make the following moves. 5B, 10C, 5C, 20B, 5A, 10B, 5B, 50C, 5C, 10A, 5A, 20C, 5B, 10C and 5C i.e. 15 moves.

Let us put these results in a table

No. of coins	Minimum no. of moves	Formula
2	3	$2^2 - 1$
3	7	$2^3 - 1$
4	15	$2^4 - 1$
5	31	$2^5 - 1$
6	63	$2^6 - 1$
n		$2^n - 1$

Banaras is a holy city in India. It seems Lord Brahma once played this trick with three sticks and gold rings. He placed the largest ring at the bottom of stick A followed by gradually reduced diameter rings one above the other into the same stick A totally numbering to 64 gold rings. He asked the priests of the temple to shift them into stick C following same rules as stated above. According to the derived formula the number of movements would have been $2^{64} - 1 = (1.844674407)^{19}$.

Suppose each movement required one second without taking time for thinking, the number of years to perform this trick by the priests would have been 584542 million years!!!

3. Karl Fredrich Gauss

The celebrated German mathematcian Karl Fredrich Gauss (1711-1855) was nine years boy and he was asked to add all the numbers from 1 to 100. Do you know how intelligently he did it? See below.

1 + 2 + 3 + ... + 98 + 99 + 100 - - - - - - - (1)

100+99+ 97 + ... + 3 + 2 + 1 - - - - - - - (2)

He added the two series (101 X 100) and dividing by 2 he got the answer as 5,050.

4. One billion problem

Now can you find the sum of all digits in the numbers from 1 to 1,000,000,000. (10^9 = one billion) That is *all the digits* in all the numbers, not all the numbers themselves

5. Chess smart

Chess game was first started in India. It was invented by a teacher known as 'Chetta'. One day the king, Sherram called him and announced that he is very much pleased by the invention of the game and wished to give presents to Chetta. "Ask whatever you want to ask me. Do not hesitate. I possess everything in this world" said the proud king magnanimously. The old man Chetta bowed to the king and said, " O Lord, your love is boundless. Please ask your servants to make huge, large size chessboard in the open yard lawn. Let them place one wheat grain in the first square, two grains in the second square, four grains in the third square, eight grains in the fourth square, sixteen in the fifth square, thirty two in the sixth square...."

The king got tired to listen, "Stop, you are very meagre in asking this humble present. I will give you as you are requesting by filling each square with grains as double as were in the previous one."

After this the king forgot his promise. Two days have gone. He asked his minister about the arrangements. The minister told him that servants and all the people in the state are busy in filling the squares. They filled only 32 squares. All the wheat stock is finished. We are requesting wheat on loan from next countries. This was the reply from the minister that shocked the king!

Can you workout how much of grains are required to fill all the 64 squares of the chessboard.

6. Biggest number using ones.

What is the biggest number one can write using four '1's?

7. Again rumours.

Referring problem 1 with same conditions, suppose I tell the secret message of my Lotto winning to ten people instead of three how many people in the town will know the message between 9 to 9-30 AM?

8. A profitable deal.

Once there were a very rich multi-billionaire but a great miser and also not well educated. One day a smart clever girl approached him and made a deal.

"Tomorrow is April 1st and I will give you £100,000 and in turn you must give me only 1 penny. Second day again I will give you £100,000 and you give me 2 pence. Third day again I will give you £100,000 and in return give me 4 pence. Like this every day till the end of this month i.e. 30th April I will give you £100,000 and you give me number of pence twice what you gave me the previous day" the smart little girl made this proposal. Mr. Miser can not believe his ears!

"So totally you are going to pay me £3,000,000 and how are you going to get this much of money?" he questioned the girl.

"My father is getting bank loan, but you don't worry. Promise is a promise. Please make agreement deed and keep ready tomorrow. I will come with £100,000 and we both have to sign it before the Solicitor." said the girl.

The man thought that she is going to make 'an April fool of him'. But next day morning the girl came promptly and gave £100,000 and got 1p form the miser.

After one week he counted all the £700,000 notes and checked whether they are real and genuine notes. In turn he had given her

$1 + 2 + 4 + 8 + 16 + 32 + 64 = £1$ and 27p only! He was extremely happy.

"O, God You are making me more and more wealthy! I am a fool, I could have made this deal for more than one month" this was how he was feeling.

Three weeks have gone. On the 21st day he had received so far £2,100,000 from the girl but he got alarmed that he had given her totally £20971.51; but still this is less than what he had received and any how he can not break the deal. Now, if this goes on steadily till 30th April how much money the miser is fooled off otherwise, how much the little girl is profited?

9. What length is it?

Suppose I remove the entire square millimetre from a square meter and put them one next to another to form a single line what will be its length? Do this mentally.

10.   What height will it be?

Suppose I remove the entire cubic millimetres from a cube of one metre side and put them one above the other like a pillar what height will it be? Of course do it mentally.

11.   Food packets for Tsunami affected people.

One packet of food weighs 89.4 gms. One million of similar packets are exported to the Tsunami affected area. What will be the total weight in metric tons?

12.   Around the earth.

Suppose it is possible for me to walk around the earth to make a great circle about its centre, what will be the difference between the circumference of the circular track traced by my top of head and feet. Assume that I am 175 cm tall.

13.   Winning the Lotto!

In the National lottery coupon there are five columns of numbers starting from 1 up to 49. You have to tick any six numbers and pay £1 for each attempt of winning the chance of one million pounds. How many attempts I have to make to be 100% sure of becoming a millionaire?

14.   The ages of man.

Geologists divide the long span of prehistoric events into the following groups.

- Palaeolithic age – Old stone age – 3,000,000 ~ 8000 BC
- Mesolithic age – Middle stone age – 8000 ~ 2700 BC
- Neolithic age – New stone age – 2700 ~ 1900 BC
- Bronze age – 1990 ~ 500 BC
- Iron age – 500 ~ 51 BC.

15.   Space neighbours.

The nearest stars beyond Sun are of the Alpha Centauri System which is more than 4 light years away. If you drive your car at a constant speed of 88 km/h you could reach Sun in 193 years. But at this same speed you may reach the nearest point in this star galaxy in 52×10^6 (52 million) years!

16.   Giant Universe.

- Every point on the equator of our earth is moving at about 1,600 km/h. The annual journey of earth around the Sun is at about 107,000 km/h.

- Our galaxy – Milky Way spins around its own axis completing one revolution for every 230 million years and moves at 792,000 km/h.
- With the modern technology the critical distance for the boundary of the observable universe – though not necessarily the boundary – is believed to be about 1, 5000 million light years from the earth.
- The temperature of the Sun at the centre is about 15,000,000°C.

17.   Our Solar System.

Our earth is one of the nine planets orbiting the Sun that together make up the solar system. The planets in order of their distance from the Sun are tabulated below.

Planet	Diameter of its equator In km.	Distance from Sun In km	Its own moons	Rotation –own axis – earth time	Orbiting Sun – earth days
Mercury	4900	58 x 10^6	No	59 days	88
Venus	12,100	108 x 10^6	No	243.4 days	225
Earth	12,756	150 x 10^6	0ne	24 hours	365.25
Mars	6800	142 x 10^6	Two	25 hours	687
Jupiter	143,000	778 x 10^6	sixteen	10 hours	11.86
Saturn	120,000	1,427 x 10^6	Seventeen	10.25 hours	29.46
Uranus	52,000	2,870 x 10^6	Five	16 ~ 20 hours	84
Neptune	48,000	4,500 x 10^6	Three	18 ~ 20 hours	165
Pluto	3,000	5,970 x 10^6	One	6.4 days	248

Note: Venus is the only planet in the Solar system that rotates from east to west while all other planets rotate from west to east. For this planet the time to take to go round the Sun is less than to rotate about its own axis. Therefore the Venusian day is longer than the Venusian year!

18.   Counting the countless.

The British Astronomer Sir Arthur Eddington (1882 – 1944) once estimated that the total number of fundamental particles in the entire Universe came to only 10^{89} i.e. the number 1 followed by 89 zeros. Mathematicians have, however developed to count numbers even larger than this. For example the number 10^{100} is named as one googol by the US mathematician, Edward Kasner of 20th century. This idea was given to him by his 13 year old son! The largest named number is 10^{googol} or the figure 1 with 10^{100} zeros after it. It is known as googolplex. But this giant of giant number can never be written down fully in a paper because there are not enough particles in the Universe to carry all the zeros!

19.   Counting and counting

If a person starts counting at the rate of 100 numbers per minute for 8 hours a day and five days in a week, it will take little over 4 weeks to count one million and just over 80 years to count 1000 millions that we call as one billion!

Archimedes (287 – 212 BC). He was one of the first to apply scientific thinking to everyday problems. He gave proofs for finding area, volume and centre of gravity of circles, spheres, conics and spirals. He gave the value of Π as $3\frac{10}{71} < \Pi < 3\frac{10}{70}$.

He conducted experiments on specific gravity and buoyancy. He was killed in the siege of Syracuse at the age of 75.

Answers: Giant numbers

4. The numbers are grouped by pairs as Gauss did.

999,999,999 + 1

999,999,998 + 2

999,999,997 + 3, and so on. There are half a billion pairs and sum of all digits in each pair is 81. The digit sum in the unpaired number 1,000,000,000 is 1. Hence the total sum will be (500,000,000 X 81) + 1 = 40,500,000,001.

5. 2^{64}-1 = 1,84,467,440,737,095,516,151.If we cultivate wheat on all the lands including ocean surface successfully even then it won't be enough to meet this demand. Suppose we make a prismoidal box of 1m x 1m and of length twice the distance from earth to Sun.it may just hold this much of wheat grains!

6. Everyone will say 1,111 but that is not the answer! The biggest giant number is 11^{11}. If you try to solve this by using logarithms you may find the answer is grater than 28 crores. i.e. 280,000,000,000.

7. Workout as explained in problem 1. You will get that by 9-30AM about 1,111,111 people i.e. even people of neighbouring towns will get the message of my Lotto winning!

8. This is again a geometric series. The girl spent £3,000,000 and the man had given $2^{30} - 1 - 1073741823$ pence or £10,737,418.23. So her profit is £7,737,418.23

9. One kilo metre.

10. Don't be shocked! It will be 1,000 kilo metre.

11. The total weight is 89.4 tons.

12. This has got nothing to do with giant numbers! The difference between to circumferences are

$$2 \times 3.14 \times (R + 175)) - 2 \times 3.14 \times R = 1,100 cm$$

13. The total money I will have to spend to be 100% sure of winning one million is 49 x 48 x 47 x 46 x 45 x 44 =

£ 10,068,347,520. i.e more than ten billion pounds.

8. MAGIC SQUARES & CROSS SUMS

1. Chinese Magic square.

4	9	2
3	5	7
8	1	6

The Chinese magic square shown on the left side dates back to 4000 years before our era!

The first nine numbers are arranged to add to 15 across each row, down each column, and along each main diagonal.

2. Indian Magic square.

1	14	15	4
12	7	6	9
8	11	10	5
13	2	3	16

The (4 × 4) order 4 magic square shown on the left side comes from India. This Indian magic square is 2000 years old. Magic squares reached Europe at the beginning of 15th century. Albert Dürer's engravings, 'Melencolia' (1514) shows a magic square similar to the 4 × 4 square from India. The 2000 years old magic square from India has the following fantastic unimaginable properties!

a) All horizontal lines add up to 34
b) All vertical lines add up to 34
c) The diagonals add up to 34
d) The four corner numbers add to 34
e) The numbers in the 2 × 2 squares in the corners and in the centre add up to 34. This sum (34) is called as the 'Magic count'.
f) In each row one pair of adjacent numbers add to 15 and the other to 19 alternatively
g) Add the squares of the numbers in each row and see the beauty of it!

$1^2 + 14^2 + 15^2 + 4^2 = 438;$ $12^2 + 7^2 + 6^2 + 9^2 = 310$

$13^2 + 2^2 + 3^2 + 16^2 = 438$ $8^2 + 11^2 + 10^2 + 5^2 = 310$

Shows that the sums of outer row pair are equal to 438 and sums of inner row pairs are equal to 310.

h) Similarly add the squares of the numbers in each vertical column and see what you get!

$1^2 + 12^2 + 8^2 + 13^2 = 378$ $14^2 + 7^2 + 11^2 + 2^2 = 370$

$4^2 + 9^2 + 5^2 + 16^2 = 378$ $15^2 + 6^2 + 10^2 + 3^2 = 370$

Shows that the sums of outer column pairs are equal to 378 and sums of inner column pairs are equal to 370.

3.   Draw on the Indian Magic square, a smaller square, as shown by broken lines. Take opposite sides in the new square. The sums are 34. See below.

$12 + 14 + 3 + 5 = 15 + 9 + 8 + 2 = 34.$

The sums of the squares and cubes of these numbers are also equal.

$12^2 + 14^2 + 3^2 + 5^2 = 15^2 + 9^2 + 8^2 + 2^2 = 374$

$12^3 + 14^3 + 3^3 + 5^3 = 15^3 + 9^3 + 8^3 + 2^3 = 4624$

4   In the Indian magic square interchange the second row numbers 12, 7, 6, 9 to the first row and the first row numbers to the second while the third and the fourth row remain the same and prepare a new magic square. Find out what properties this square has got.

5   **Six pointed star with numbers.**

Fill in the circles with numbers from 1 to 12 in the corners of the six-pointed star shown below. The sum of the numbers in each of the six lines must be 26.

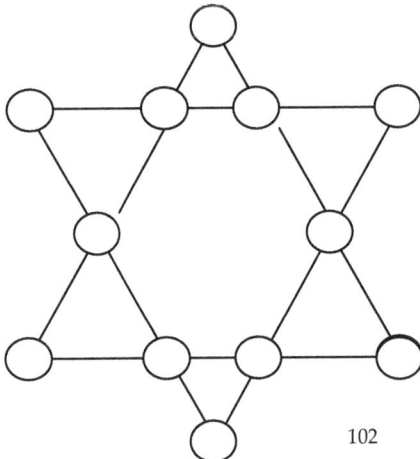

6. A square lattice grid

Thirteen players are asked to stand in the form of a lattice work as shown below. Select 13 integers in which twelve are different and ascribe to them so that each row sums to 20. The smallest is 1 and the largest is 15.

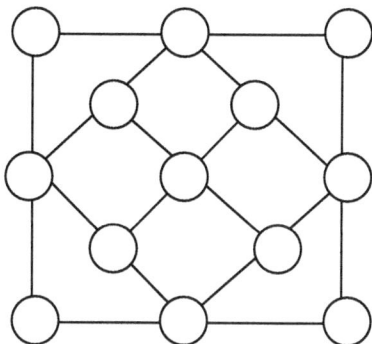

7. Hexagonal pond

A hexagonal pond is decorated with 19 colour bulbs as shown in figure. Mark the bulbs with numbers ranging from 1 to 19 so that each outer edge adds up to 22 and also each of the line from the centre to the outer corners adds to 22.

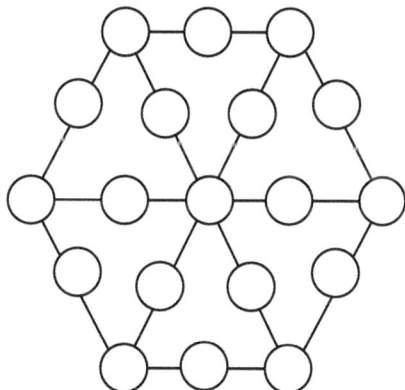

8. Attempt the hexagon pond problem of 7 satisfying same conditions but resulting the sum to 23.

9.   Cross sums 1.

Fill the square given below with numbers other than '0' satisfying the following conditions.

Across: 'a' an even number with 8 as a factor.

       'c' all are of even digits

       'd' digits all different, even and sum of the digits is 12.

Down: 'a' one odd and two even digits and sum of the digits is > 15.

       'b' even and two digits are repeated.

       'e' a perfect cube

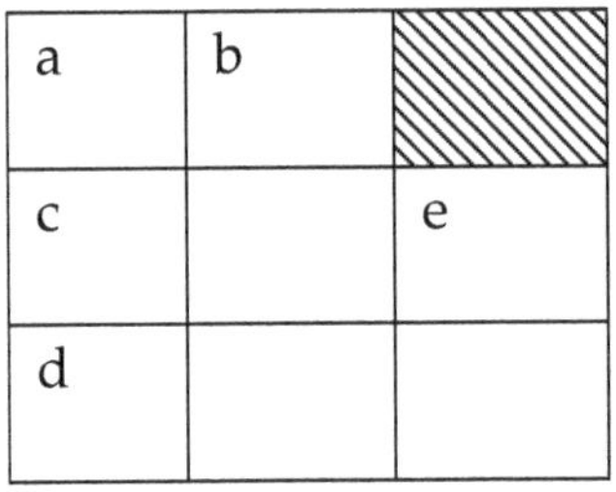

a	b	
c		e
d		

10. Cross sums 2.

For the cross number problem shown below there are no zeros. Fill the spaces to satisfy the following conditions..

Across: 'a' prime number and the unit place a factor of 3

       'c' an odd number, each digit is less than the one before.

       'd' number 'xyx' where x = 2 times the number in'a' and y = the number in the square 'a'.

Down: 'a' see 'd' across.

       'b' twice the prime number >50

       'c' twice the prime number <20

	a	b
c		
d		

11. Cross sums 3.

Fill the spaces with suitable numbers to satisfy the given conditions. There are no zeros.

Across: a) An even number in which two are repeated odd numbers.

        c) A square and even number.

        d) Reverse of row (a) the sum of the numbers being 12

Down: a) Beginning two are odd numbers with an even number at the unit place.

        b) An even number in the middle with equal odd numbers at the ends.

Diagonal a) Same as (b) down

a	b	
c		
d		

12. Cross sums 4.

Fill up the spaces for the cross number diagram given below. As usual no zeros to be used.

Across: a) The square of an odd number.

        d) The quotient when (a) is divided by 8.

        e) The same when reversed.

Down: b) All even numbers with LCM 24

c) Even and one number is repeated from row 'a'.

a	b	c
///	d	
e		

13. Cross sums 5.

In this no space is left blank and no zeros are allowed.

Across: a) Sum of digits in this row is '12'

c) Each digit is '2' less than that before.

d) A perfect square.

Down: a) The same when reversed

b) Square of natural numbers decreasing down.

d) An even number and divisible by '11'.

a		b
c	d	
	e	

14.   Cross sums 6.

Do the following cross sum.   No zeros.

Across: a) A factor of 'c' across.

c) Even number.with LCM 8

d) Cubes of natural number and same when reversed.

Down : a) The sum of digits is 15

b) Same as (d) across.

c) Ten less than (a) across.

	a	b
c		
d		

15. Preparing a 5th order magic square.

Draw the main matrix of 5 X 5 and shade it inside a 9 X 9 matrix as shown in figure down.. Enter the integers from 1 to 25 in the five diagonally slanting lines. Each integer outside the shaded matrix is moved 5 cells along its row or column into the main square. For example 6 is moved under 18, 24 over 12, 16 to the right of 8 and 4 to the left of 12. The resulting magic square is shown in

				1				
			6		2			
		11		7		3		
	16		12		8		4	
21		17		13		9		5
	22		18		14		10	
		23		19		15		
			24		20			
				25				

the next page. The magic constant is 65. The magic square is also symmetrically inserted with numbers. Each number added to its 'opposite' on the other side of the central cell in the same line is 26

$9 + 17 = 21 + 5 = 19 + 7 = 1 + 25 = 26$. The same method can be used to produce magic squares of any odd type order like 3×3, 7×7 etc.

The final, fifth order magic square is shown below.

11	24	7	20	3
4	12	25	8	16
17	5	13	21	9
10	18	1	14	22
23	6	19	2	15

16. Construction of a magic square of 4th order.

Draw a square with 4×4 cells. Number the cells in the consecutive order from 1 to 16 as shown in figure (a) below. Divide the square by shading the centre 2×2 matrix and all the four corner squares so that in each corner there is a square of order $\dfrac{n}{4} = \dfrac{4}{4} = 1$ and in the centre a square of order $\dfrac{n}{2} = \dfrac{4}{2} = 2$. Within the five squares, interchange all pairs of numbers symmetrically opposite the square's centre. Outside these five squares leave the numbers as they are. See figure (b) showing the final 4 ×4 magic square.

1	2	3	4
5	6	7	8
9	10	11	12
13	14	15	16

16	2	3	13
5	11	10	8
9	7	6	12
4	14	15	1

Figure (a)   Figure (b)

17. Construction of magic squares in the order of 'n' in any multiples of 4.

If n = 8 we have to prepare a magic square of 8th order which is a multiple 4 with 2. Draw a square with 8 × 8 cells. (n = 8). Number them from 1 to 64 in consecutive order as shown in figure (a). Divide this big square by shading so that in each corner you have mini-square of order n/4 = 8/4 = 2 and in the centre a sub-square of order n/2 = 8/2 = 4. Now you are having altogether 5 squares. As explained and shown in previous problem, interchange all pairs of numbers symmetrically opposite the centre's square. Outside these five squares leave the numbers as they are. This is the final 8 ×8 magic square and shown in figure (b).

The magic constant in any magic square is given by the formula, $C = \dfrac{n^3 + n}{2}$.

For the 8 × 8 magic square = 260

1	2	3	4	5	6	7	8
9	10	11	12	13	14	15	16
17	18	19	20	21	22	23	24
25	26	27	28	29	30	31	32
33	34	35	36	37	38	39	40
41	42	43	44	45	46	47	48
49	50	51	52	53	54	55	56
57	58	59	60	61	62	63	64

Figure (a)

64	63	3	4	5	6	56	57
56	55	11	12	13	14	50	49
17	18	46	45	44	43	23	24
25	26	38	37	36	35	31	32
33	34	30	29	28	27	39	40
41	42	22	21	20	19	47	48
16	15	51	52	53	54	10	9
8	7	59	60	61	62	2	1

Figure (b)

18. Construct a magic square of order 'n', where n is even and not a multiple of 4; say n = 6, 10 etc.

Let us consider a simple case of 6th order magic square. Construct a annular frame leaving the central 4 ×4 shaded matrix See figure. The central square is 4th order and construct magic square as explained in problem 16. Increase each number in the cells of figure (b) of problem 16 by $(2n – 2)$. In this case increase by $(2×6 – 2) = 10$. The resulting square is shown in figure is shown shaded in the central 4 ×4 matrix.

1	9	34	33	32	2
6	26	12	13	22	31
10	15	21	20	18	27
30	19	17	16	22	7
29	14	24	25	11	8
35	28	3	4	5	36

Hence, 1 becomes 11, 2 becomes 12 etc.   In the outer frame not shaded, it is always possible by guessing to place numbers 1 to 10 and 27 to 36 remembering the magic constant must be 111, (using the formula stated in the previous problem).

19. Solve the following Cross Number puzzle.

Across:

1.   Square of a prime number and also its sum.

5.   Odd number and a factor of 10 and 11 down..

6.   Cube of a square
8   A prime number and square root of 1 across.
10. A symmetrical square (same left to right as right to left)
13. Larger by 1 than 9 down.
14. Across 8 is multiplied by 5
15. Square of a number larger by one than 13 across.

Down:
1.   A number having only one factor of two odd digits.
2.   Number having two repetitions with digit sum is 29.
3.   Prime number digits differ by 2.
4.   Prime factor of 11 down.
7.   Quadrupled product of one tenth 15 across and 13 across.
9.   Twice 4 down.
10. 11 down reversed.
11. Square root of 10 across.
12. Multiple of the highest prime factor of 13 across.
13. Same as 9 down.

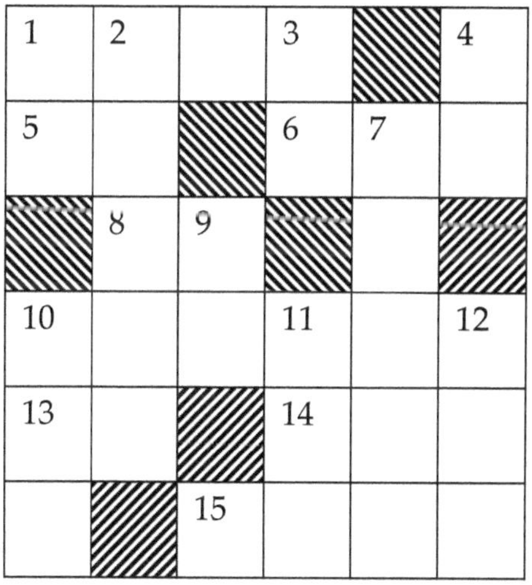

20.   Lattice frame of a glass window

The figure shows a glass paned window. It contains 16 small triangles. With a careful observation one could notice that there are 6 bigger overlapping triangles. All the triangles are right-angled type. Insert numbers from 1 to 16 inside smaller triangles such that sum of the numbers in bigger overlapping triangles is always 34.

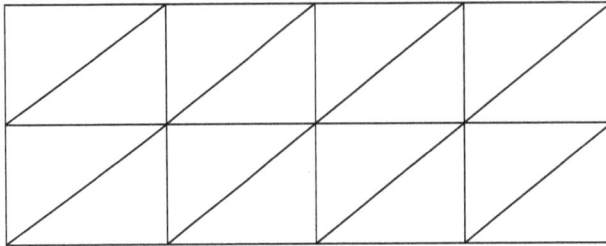

21.. Triangle with numbers adding to 20

Draw an equilateral triangle and fill on the three sides with different numbers from 1 to 9 so that their sum on each side is 20.

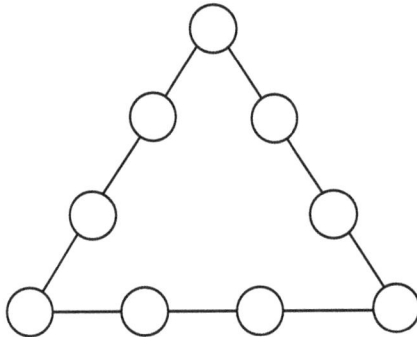

22.. Triangle with numbers adding to 17

Repeat the problem 21 with the condition that the sum of numbers on each side is 17.

23.. Numbers on a Six-corner star

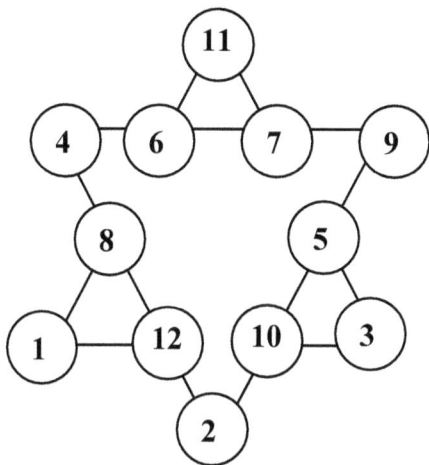

The figure shown for this problem is a peculiar one. The sum of numbers in each side is 26 but the sum of numbers on all corners is 30. Check this from the figure shown above.

24. Another six-corner star problem
Can you re-arrange the numbers on the figure of problem (23) such that sum of numbers on all sides and also sum of numbers on all corners is 26?

25. Chessboard squares
Everybody knows the Chessboard. This may not be a simple question. Can any one tell how many squares are there altogether? Mind it is not 64.

26. Numbers on the dial face of a table clock.
Can you divide the face of the clock shown into six sections so that each section will have the numbers within the section adding to the same value?

27. Peculiar magic square.

In a big cardboard prepare the square of 4 × 4 order and fill it with numbers as shown in following.

10	6	9	13
8	4	7	1
14	10	13	17
9	5	8	12

You may require four of friends to perform this game. Let A crosses a row and a column of his choice with red pencil. B crosses any remaining row and column with blue colour. Similarly C does with brown colour and D crosses the left over row and column with green colour. Ask them to add all the numbers intersected by the four colours and it will be always 39! For example $R_1C_4 + R_2C_2 + R_3C_1 + R_4C_3 = 13 + 4 + 14 + 8 = 39$

Let us see the method to prepare this strange magic square. Prepare a 5th order matrix and enter the outer row and column by numbers as shown below.

8	4	7	11	
10				2
	4			0
		13		6
			12	1

114

Now add the numbers in R_1 and C_1 and fill in grid (a) i.e. 10 similarly fill all the grids. As a sample the diagonal grids are filled and shown above.

28. Can you prepare magic square of 4 x 4 order like the one shown above in which the numbers corresponding to the intersecting colour lines add up to 47.

29. Determinant of 3rd order Magic square.

Let S be the sum of integers in the 3rd order Chinese magic square and let D be the value of its determinant show that D/S is an integer whose value is 8.

4	9	2
3	5	7
8	1	6

The Chinese magic square is shown above. S = 3 times the magic constant = 45.
D = 4 (30 – 7) – 9 (18 – 56) + 2 (3 – 40) = 360.
D/S = 360 / 45 = 8. Proved.

30. Triangle with missing numbers.

Refer to the first triangle given below. You will notice that the average of the numbers at the vertices of each side is the corresponding middle number.

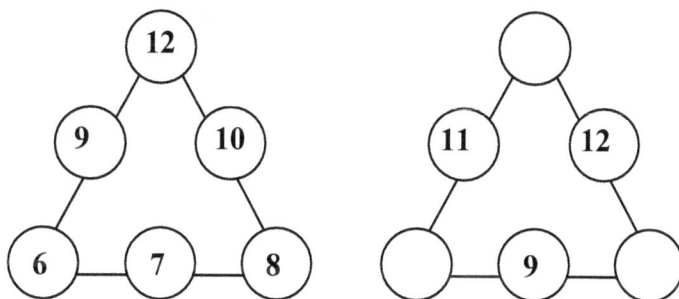

Using the same principle can you find the numbers on the vertices of the second figure?

31. Dart board.

Mr. Dartwell wants to score exactly 100 points with throwing of four darts on the board. What are the aims he has to make on the board shown below?

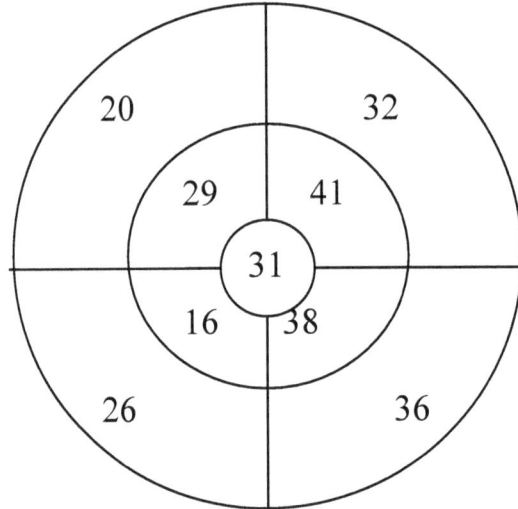

32. Magic squares of Planets

Like astrology, numerology is also an art of forecasting one's life events. In Hindu tradition both of these scientific practices had been followed right from ancient periods. Planets of Solar system had been assigned with magic squares. Magic square of each planet is given below. One's date of birth, day of birth and position of their birth sign like Scorpio, Capricorn etc. are taken into account. The magic constant given below are also important to forecast the future, to fix or change the names or to assign lucky numbers and so on.

6	1	8
7	5	3
2	9	4

Magic square of Sun:. The magic constant is 15. (1 + 5 = 6). Planet Sun number is 6

7	2	9
8	6	4
3	10	5

Magic square of Moon: The magic constant is 18 (1 + 8 = 9). Moon's number is 9.

8	3	10
9	7	5
4	11	6

Magic square of Mars: The magic constant is 21 (2 + 1 = 3).
Mars' number is 3

9	4	11
10	8	6
5	12	7

Magic square of Mercury: The magic constant is 24 (2 + 4 = 6).
Mercury's number is 6

10	5	12
11	9	7
6	13	8

Magic square of Jupiter: The magic constant is 27 (2 + 7 = 9).
Jupiter's number is 9

11	6	13
12	10	8
7	14	9

Magic square of Venus: The magic constant is 30 (3 + 0 = 3).
Venus number is 3.

12	7	14
13	11	9
8	15	10

Magic square of Saturn: The magic constant is 33 (3 + 3 = 6).
Saturn's number is 6.

13	8	15
14	12	10
9	16	11

Magic square of Dragon's head (Raghu): The magic constant
is 36 (3 + 6 = 9). Raghu's number is 9..

14	9	16
15	13	11
10	17	12

Magic square of Dragon's tail (Kedhu): The magic constant is
39 (3 + 9 = 1 + 2 = 3). Kedhu's number is 3.

Let us consider the name of an imaginary person, say, Mr. Michael and analyse how these planets affect his life events and how the alphabets in his name influence good or bad. According to numerology the following numbers are assigned to alphabets.

(A, I, J, Q, Y)---1;   (B, K, R)----2;   (C, G, L, S)----3
(D, M, T)----- 4   (E, H, N, X)---5   (U, V, W)--- 6
(O, Z)   ---- 7   (F, P) ----8

The general qualities of this person according to numerology can be said as follows:

"He is always keen and enthusiastic, possessing high mental strength, successful completion of his attempts and he is straight forward.   He will be having less number of friends.   He doesn't believe the words of others.   He wishes to enjoy the pleasures of the world, pride and wealth but in his later life he will turn to be more spiritual and public related.   His number is 22.   Mars, Venus, Moon and Mercury are his favourite planets.   According to horoscope if he is born in Taurus as birth sign it will be better for him to start any events like business, buying property etc.   during the period when the above said planets prevail in good aspects.   Sun, Jupiter, Raghu and Kedhu are the weak planets to him. Astrology and Numerology are vast fields and details are beyond the scope of this book.

Ramanujam (1887 – 1920). One of India's greatest mathematicians. Son of a Hindu Brahmin who worked as a clerk. The following are a few of his famous inventions. Solutions for cubic equations, Euler's constant and Bernoullis numbers, elliptic functions, continued fractions and divergent series. He collaborated with Prof. Hardy of Trinity College, Cambridge in 1914. He got PhD award from Cambridge in 1916 and elected as the Fellow of Royal Society of Maths.

Answers: Magic squares and Cross sums

4. You will notice that this new square exhibits the following properties.
The magic count of the rows is 34 and for the columns are also 34.
But the sum of main diagonal numbers is different.
The sum of the squares of the diagonal numbers is same.   The sum of cubes of
the diagonal numbers is same.

5.   Top: 9; second row: 4, 7, 10, 5; third row: 8 and 6; fourth row: 2, 11, 12, 1
and the bottom corner 3.

6.   Outer corners in clockwise 11, 5, 5 and 8.   In between 11 and 5 is 4; between 5
and 5 is 10; between 5 and 8 is 7; between 8 and 11 is 1.   For the inner square
between 4 and 10 is 6; 10 and 7 is 3; 7 and 1 is 12 and between 1 and 4 is 15.   The
centre number is 2.

7.   From top of hexagon, row 1 is 1, 18, 3.   Row 2 is 14, 19, 17, 15.   Middle row is
7, 13, 2, 16, 4.   Row 4 is 6, 11, 12, 10.   Bottom row is 9, 5, 8.

8.   From top of hexagon, row 1 is 1, 19, 3.   Row 2 is 18, 16, 14, 12.   Middle row is
4, 13, 6, 9, 8.   Row 4 is 17, 15, 7, 5.   Bottom row is 2, 11, 10.

9.   First row 'ab' = 72;   second row starting with 'c' is 486; third row starting
with 'd' is624.

10..   : Row starting with 'a' = 41.   Row starting with 'c' = 321.   Row starting with
'd' = 848..

11.   First row is 336.   Second row is16.   Third row is 633.

12.   Row 'a' = 169.   Row 'd' = 21.   Row 'e' = 484

13.   Row 1 with 'a' = 129.   Row 2 with 'c' = 864.   Row 3 = 161.

14.   Row with 'a' = 31.   Row with 'c' = 248.   Row with 'd' = 181.

19. Across: 1 – 5329; 5 – 11; 6 - 729; 8 – 73; 10 – 698,896; 13 – 39; 14 – 365; 15 – 1600
Down: 1 – 51; 2 – 31,799; 3 – 97; 4 – 19; 7 – 24,960; 9 – 38; 10 – 638; 11 – 836; 12 – 650.

20. Top row: 1 / 16; 9 /15; 3 / 14; 11 / 13
Bottom row: 8 / 2; 7 /10; 6/ 4; 5/ 12.

21. (5, 3, 4, 8); (8, 1, 9, 2); (2, 6, 7, 5)

22. (2, 4, 8, 3); (3, 7, 6, 1); (1, 9, 5, 2)

24. Top corner of the six-star is 10; bottom corner is 3; below 10 , the horizontal row is 4, 7, 9 and 6; the middle row is 8, 5; the horizontal row above 3 is 1, 11, 12, 2.

25. There are 64 numbers of 1 × 1 squares; 49 of 2 × 2 squares, 36 of 3 × 3 squares etc. up to the outer frame of 1 × 1 biggest square. $8^2 + 7^2 + 6^2 + 5^2 + 4^2 + 3^2 + 2^2 + 1^2 = 204$.

26. Refer to the figure of clock on the next page. Numbers within the six sections add to 13.

28.

10	6	12	4	
17	13	19	11	7
10	6	12	4	0
13	9	15	7	3
15	11	17	9	5

30. Try with numbers 14, 10 and 8.

31. Zones marked with scores 16, 20, 26 and 38.

Albert Einstein (1879 – 1955). Worked as the patent office clerk in Berne. He put forward his famous theory of relativity in 1905 based on the fact that the velocity of light is absolute. The mass, length and even time can only be measured relative to the observer and undergo transformation when studied by another observer. His formula $E = mC^2$ laid the foundation to nuclear physics, a fact that he deplore in its application to warfare. In 1933 he moved from Nazi Germany to settle in America.

9

NUMBER MAGIC

I have often admired the mystical way of Pythagoras and the secret magic of numbers.

Sir Thomas Browne

One, two, buckle my shoe,
Three, four, shut the door,
Five, six pick up the sticks,
Seven, eight lay them straight,
Nine, ten, a good fat hen,
Eleven, twelve dig and delve,
Thirteen, fourteen, go to canteen,
Fifteen, sixteen, dine in the kitchen,
Seventeen, eighteen, we are waiting,
Nineteen, twenty, our plates are empty.

1.   Number, animal, country.

Think of a number between 1 and 10, including 1 and 10. Multiply your number by 9 and add the digits of the number you got after multiplying by nine. Subtract 5 from the previous result.. Select the letter in the alphabet that suits to the number from the above step. Like A for 1, B for 2, C for 3 etc...Pick a country in Europe that starts with letter you had chosen in the above step. Pick an animal that starts with the last letter of the country you had picked up above; Pick a colour that starts with the last letter of your animal. Now I will tell the answer as

"Denmark, kangaroo and orange". Am I right? Do not try this trick more than once, because the answer will be always the same!

2. Select a number from the grid.

To perform this game you have to prepare the following seven grids of numbers in a cardboard. Cut them separately and spread on a table. Ask your friend to think of any number between 1 to 99 (inclusive of 1 and 99). Ask him to look at the cards and give you back every card that has his chosen number on it. As Soon as he had done this you can tell exactly what number he had thought!

2	3	6	7	10	11	14	15
18	19	22	23	26	27	30	31
34	35	38	39	42	43	46	47
50	51	54	55	58	59	62	63
66	67	70	71	74	75	78	79
82	83	86	87	90	91	94	95
98	99						

4	5	6	7	12	13	14	15
20	21	22	23	28	29	30	31
36	37	38	39	44	45	46	47
52	53	54	55	60	61	62	63
68	69	70	71	76	77	78	79
84	85	86	87				

64	65	66	67	68	69	70	71
72	73	74	75	76	77	78	79
80	81	82	83	84	85	86	87
88	89	90	91	92	93	94	95
96	97	98	99				

8	9	10	11	12	13	14	15
24	25	26	27	28	29	30	31
40	41	42	43	44	45	46	47
56	57	58	59	60	61	62	63
72	73	74	75	76	77	78	79
88	89	90	91	92	93	94	95

1	3	5	7	9	11	13	15
17	19	21	23	25	27	29	31
33	35	37	39	41	43	45	47
49	51	53	55	57	59	61	63
65	67	69	71	73	75	77	79
81	83	85	87	89	91	93	95
97	99						

16	17	18	19	20	21	22	23
24	25	26	27	28	29	30	31
48	49	50	51	52	53	54	55
56	57	58	59	60	61	62	63
80	81	82	83	84	85	86	87
88	89	90	91	92	93	94	95

32	33	34	35	36	37	38	39
40	41	42	43	44	45	46	47
48	49	50	51	52	53	54	55
56	57	58	59	60	61	62	63
96	97	98	99				

Just add the number in the top left-hand corner in every card he gives you back in which his chosen number appear. If 97 is his chosen number, the left-hand corner number in the cards returned back to you will be 1 + 32 + 64 = 97.

3.   Going to St. Paul's church

As I was going to St. Paul's church I met an old man with six wives. Every wife had six children and every child had six dogs and every dog had six puppies. Puppies, dogs, children and wives, how many were going to St. Paul's?

4. Think of a number.

Subtract 1 from it and double the result. Add the thought number to the result. Tell me the final answer and I will tell you the number you thought!

Suppose you thought 17. Subtract 1 and it becomes 16. Double it, 2 x 16 = 32. Add the thought number, 32 + 17 = 49. And you will be telling me 49 and immediately I will tell that you thought 17! How?

5. Same as 2

This magic is similar to No. 2. Here, instead of seven tabulations we combine everything into a single table.

A	B	C	D	E
1	2	4	8	16
7	31	28	12	30
15	26	6	15	26
31	19	30	9	28
3	23	14	28	17
9	15	31	26	20
17	6	29	11	29
5	14	7	31	23
11	3	5	14	21
13	30	20	13	31
21	18	13	27	22
19	11	21	30	24
23	22	12	25	18
27	7	23	10	25
25	27	15	24	27
29	10	22	29	19

Ask your friend choose any one number from any one of the five columns. Question him whether it appears in column A or B etc. Add mentally the top numbers of the respective columns he says to you. The answer is the number he has chosen.

Example: Suppose he selects 27, it appears in columns A, B, D and E. The corresponding top row numbers are 1, 2, 8 and 16. The sum of these numbers is 27 that he has chosen!

6. Read from the calculator

Try the following calculations using 8 or 10 digit calculator. Find results and turn your calculator for each result you got and try to read what it means!

a) 4.40 x 700 = musical instrument
b) 2.17 x 12100 – 8550 = A kind of 'pop'.
c) 2.101 x 1.8 = A holy book
d) $7.964^2 + 7.652049$ = An oil company
e) $7.11 \times 10^6 – 9447$ = An oil corporation
f) 1.59 x 35700 – 19025 = A beautiful young lady

g)   47.1 x 2650 + 410699 = What a snake does
h)   0.31 x 110² = A small island
i)   50.16 x 1100 + 2542 = Unwelcome arrival during the first week of every month.
j)   [(1089 +200) ÷ 10,000] x 6 = Just a word of greeting to my friend.

7.   Some more calculator puzzles.
Here are some more words that turn into numbers in your calculator as stated above. Create suitable mathematical steps to arrive at these numbers in your calculator and turn and see what words they signify.
7714, 7735, 637, 7738, 663, 715, 3807, 3704, 604, 3705, 5507 and 5537.

8.   Christmas presents
Our Church Executive committee was arranging a Christmas tree. After distributing sweets and cakes in the gift packets, we began to put oranges in each packet. Before that we calculated that if we put 10 oranges to a package, one package would only get 9; if we put 9 oranges to a packet, one would get only 8. Like that if 8 then one would get only 7; if 7 one would get 6 and so on till if two oranges per package the last would have only one. How many oranges we had in the beginning?

9.   Find the number
My father bought a box of balloons for my birth day. I wanted to put them in bags and distribute to my friends. If I put three in a bag finally one balloon remains; if it is 4 in a bag 2 remains; 5 in a bag means 3 remains and 6 in a bag makes 4 balloons left-over. How many balloons were there originally in the box?

10.   Complete the equation
The temperature of a place is represented in absolute scale by the following equation where, t is the temperature in Celsius and x is an integer. Find the value of t and the digit symbolised by x. in the equation $[3(270+t)]^2 = 74x,496$.

11.   Mrs. Peacock's family
Mrs. Peacock has 2 children. They are not both boys. What is the probability that both the children are girls?

12.   Mr. Smith has two children.
The eldest is a boy. What is the probability that both children are boys?

13. Flips, Flops and Flubs

All Flips are Flops and all Flops are Flubs. 80% of the Flubs are Flops and 80% of the Flops are Flips. What percentage of the Flubs are Flops but are not Flips?

14. Random operation of a guessed number

Ask your friend to think of a number. Tell him to multiply or divide by several numbers which you call out at random, without telling you the result. No additions or subtractions. Then ask him to divide by the 'thought' number and then add the 'thought' number. Finally when he tells his result you can immediately figure out the 'thought' number.

15. Think an even number

Say it is 48. Add half of it. 48 + 24 = 72. Add half this sum. 72 + 36 = 108. Divide it by nine and you get 12. The thought number is four times the quotient. Let us see how it works. If the thought number is 'x' then

$x + x/2 = 3x/2$, $(3x/2 + 3x/4) = 9x/4$. Dividing this by 9 and multiplying with 4 gives back 'x'.

16. In case the thought number n, is odd

Then half of (n + 1) is called the larger part of n. Let us try problem with an odd number. Say 73. Larger part of 73 is half of 73 + 1 which is 37. Add 73 and 37, 73 + 37 = 110. Add to this half of the sum. 110 + 55 = 165. Divide by 9 which gives 18 as quotient and 3 as remainder. In the last problem the remainder was 0. But if the remainder exists consider the following rule. Add to four times the quotient
0 if the remainder is 0
1 if the remainder is less than 5
2 if the remainder is exactly 5
3 if the remainder is greater than 5
Hence, 4 x 18 + 1 = 73.

17. Think a number from 1 to 99

Ask your friend to think of a number anything from 1 to 99. Ask him to square it. Now you announce a number and ask him to add to the thought number and square it. Ask him to find the difference between these two squares and let him announce the answer. To get the 'thought number' divide half of the answer by the added number and subtract the half of the announced number. Example: Suppose he thinks 53, square of 53 is 2809. Suppose you announce 6 to be added to the thought number, 53 + 6 = 59. Square of 59 is 3481. The difference, 3481 − 2809 = 672. Half of 672 is 336 and divide by the added number, 336 / 6 = 56. Take away half of announced number, 56 −(half of 6) = 53. Let us see how this works.

Let the thought number is 'x' then above stated steps work out to x, x^2, x + a, $(x + a)^2 - x^2 = 2ax + a^2$, half of this divided by 'a' gives ½ (2x + a) and subtracting ½ a gives back x.

18. Think a number from 6 to 60: Ask your friend to think of a number from 6 to 60. Ask him to divide the thought number by 3, 4 and 5 separately and in each time whatever remainder he gets has to be announced to you. Then you do the following calculation secretly using a calculator. $(40 r_3 + 45 r_4 + 36 r_5)$. Divide this answer by 60. The remainder you get is his thought number. Example. 14 is his number. When he divides 14 by 3, 4, 5 he gets 2, 2 and 4 as remainders respectively. You workout (40x2 + 45x2 + 36x4) = 314. Divide 314 by 60 and the remainder is 14, and that is his thought number.

19. No questions, but tell your friend's result. Ask him to think any number and multiply by 4. Then he must add 15. Suppose he thinks 6, he will be getting 6 x 4 + 15 = 39. Tell him to divide the answer by 3. 39 ÷ 3 = 13. So far you have not asked him any questions. Meanwhile in your head divide the first number you supplied, 4 by 3 i.e. 4 ÷ 3 = 1 and 1/3. Now tell him to subtract thought number times 1 and 1/3 i.e. 6 x 4/3 = 8 from the answer previously he got. 13 – 8 = 5. This one also he is not announcing but you can get this by dividing second number you told him by three i.e. 15 ÷ 3 = 5. The numbers you supplied to him need not to be the same as 4, 15 and 3. It can be any thing you choose; but remember what numbers you have supplied. Check the answer section for how it works.

20. Picking any numbers from 51 to 100. Each of your friends picks a thought number from 51 to 100. In turn you as the number magician write any number from 1 to 50 and seal it in an envelope. In your mind subtract your number in the envelope from 99. Announce the result and tell the spectators to add it to their thought number, cross out the first digit of the sum and add the same crossed out digit to the result. The answer is to be subtracted from their thought number. The resulting figure is the number hiding in the sealed envelope!

21. Toy telephone. Schwetha and her sister, Ashvanthi wanted to make a toy phone. She asked her mum for a bundle of twine thread. "What happened to the bundle that I gave you yesterday?" mum questioned. "Mum you took half of it for hanging clothes and dad had taken half of the remaining bundle" replied Schwetha. Ashvanthi added "I used half of the remaining bundle to tie my old books and two fifth of the leftover were used in the garden" At the end they were having only 30cm long thread. How can they play telephone game with it? What were the length of thread originally in the bundle?

22. Socks and gloves: A box contains ten pairs of brown socks and ten pairs of black socks. Another identical box has ten pairs of brown gloves and ten pairs of black gloves. I want to take by closing my eyes, same colour of socks and gloves at the same time from these two boxes. How many of them I have to take?

23.   Salary and over-time allowance. Mr. Brown received £ 5000 as his present month pay. This also includes his over time allowance. His basic salary is £4000 greater than the over time allowance. What is his basic salary?

24. Grandpa and TV programmes: Grandpa wishes to watch TV programmes from 6 PM to 9 PM because he can not tolerate his sleep after 9 PM. One film show lasts for 80 minutes, two successive serials last for an hour each. He always forgets the exact starting time of each programme and he doesn't know how to record them into a video tape. What is the least number of minutes he will have to miss the programmes?

25. Guessing the ages of sister and brother. Once I asked my friend Tanya to add her age with her brother's age. Also I asked her to multiply their ages and adding this product to the sum with an addition of one to the result. .I asked her to tell me the final result and to her surprise I was able to tell her the ages. For example if their ages are 7 and 5 then $(7 \times 5) + (7 + 5) + 1 = 35 + 12 + 1 = 48$. Now I can tell their ages, but how? Check answer at the back.

26. Think of several single digit numbers. Think several single digit numbers. Multiply the first by 2 and add 5, multiply this answer by 5 and add 10. Add the second thought number and multiply by 10; add the third thought number and multiply by 10 and so on until finally you add the last thought number. .Now, tell me the final result and how many numbers you originally thought. For example if you had thought of 3, 9, 8 and 2 then $3 \times 2 + 5 = 11$; $11 \times 5 + 10 = 65$; $65 + 9 = 74$; $74 \times 10 = 740$; $740 + 8 = 748$; $748 \times 10 = 7480$; $7480 + 2 = 7482$. Now, I can tell all the numbers thought by you!

27. Beauty of the Magic numbers 3, 7, 11, 13 and 37.
a) We need a calculator for this game. Ask your friend to enter any number between 100 and 1000 in the calculator. Ask him to multiply his chosen number by 7, 11 and 13 one after another successively. He will get his three digits chosen number repeated once more! This is the one of the properties of 3, 7, 11.and 13.
b) Now ask him to enter any single digit number in the calculator. Ask him to multiply by 3 and 37 in any order he likes. He will get his chosen number repeated thrice!

c) Once again let him enter any single digit number in his calculator. Ask him to multiply it by 3, 7, 11, 13 and finally by 37. He will be getting a six digits number which is a repetition of his selected number six times!

28. Tom's age.
Tom is studying in primary 1 and he is a cute little boy. If his age is increased by 3 years it gives perfect integral square number. But, if his age is decreased by 3 years it gives the square root of previous result. What is Tom's age now?

29. Smart ducklings.
There were few ducklings swimming in the pond. My little grand daughter threw a peanut into the water. Half of them swam away and after five minutes ten of them returned back. The little girl once again threw a peanut into the water and again half of them went away and in five minutes ten of them returned back. For the third time also she threw a peanut at them. Again half of them went away and after same five minutes ten of them returned back. To my surprise there was the same number of ducklings in the pond. How many ducklings were there originally in the pond?

30. Animal magic.
Give instructions to your friend as follows.
* Think a number between 1 and 10. Don't tell me.
* Multiply by nine.
* I know your answer is a digit number. If it is 'ab' then add a + b.
* Take away 4 from a + b.
* Now turn this number into an alphabet. Like 1 is A, 2 is B, 3 is C, etc.
* Think of an animal with your letter.
* The animal you thought …. Elephant. Is it not!

31. Unaltered Age.
If the age of Helen is reduced by 7 and then multiplied by same 7 it remains the same as when her age is reduced by 11 and then multiplied by 11. Find the present age of my daughter's friend, Miss. Helen.

32. Six(ty) / tea cups.
Tom had six tea / sixty cups in the cupboard. Jerry broke one of them How many is remaining? If you say 5 you are wrong. Or if you say fifty nine still you are wrong.

33. Mental maths tests.
One day our maths teacher asked the following questions.
a)   By how much 40 is larger than 32?
By 8 was the answer.
b)   By how much 32 is smaller than 40?
By 8 was the answer.
c)   By what percentage 40 is larger than 32?
By 25 percent was the answer.
d)   By what percentage 32 is smaller than 40?
By 25 percent was the answer and the teacher immediately told that it is wrong!
What is the correct answer?

34. Income and purchasing capacity.
a) Suppose my monthly income increases by 25 percent by what percentage my purchasing capacity will increase?
b) Suppose my monthly income does not change but the government is considerable to reduce the prices of all commodities by 25 percent then what will be my purchasing capacity?

35. Toy shop announces sale price.
Because of year end the toy shop announced 10 percent reduction in prices and consequently it made 8 percent profit on each toy sold. What was the profit before the reduction?

36. Boosting up of working capacity.
A worker in a cycle factory reduces the protection time per part by 25 percent. How much does he increase his productivity?

37. Percentage passes.
Three schools in an area obtained the following passes in the recent Advanced level examinations. Find the percentage of passes in that area.

School	Total appeared	Passes	% passes
A	40	36	90
B	100	71	71
C	80	60	75

Answers: Number Magic

3. The answer is none! I was going to St. Paul's and others were going away from St. Paul's.

4. Always add 2 to the final answer and divide by 3. In general if x is the thought number then
(x – 1) 2 + x = 3x – 2. When you add 2 and divide by 3 the result is x.

6. a) Obae, b) Lollipop, c) Bible, d) Shell oil, e) Esso oil, f) Belle, g) hisses, h) Isle, i) Bills, j) hello.

7. Hill, Sell. Leg. Bell. Egg. Sil. Lobe. Hole. Hog. Sole. Loss. Less.

8.   With one more orange to what we had in the beginning it would have been divisible by 10, 9, 8, ….. The LCM of a set of distinct prime factors, each is taken the greatest number of times that it occurs in any one number. For example the LCM for numbers 1 to 10 is 2 x 2 x 2 x 3 x 3 x 5 x7 = 2,520. Hence we had 2520 – 1 = 2519 oranges.

9. The difference between divisor and remainder is always 2. The LCM of 3,4,5 and 6 is 60. Hence the smallest answer is 60 – 2 = 58. The general answer is (60n – 2) where n is any integer.

10. The left side of the equation is divisible by 9, so also the right side must be. It follows that the sum of 7 + 4 + x + 4 + 9 + 6 = 30 + x must be divisible by 9. X must be 6 and t = 18°C..

11. One third

12. One half.

13. Prepare a 'Venn' diagram. Answer is 16%

14. How it works? You start with 1 and do all the operations that you have asked him to do. No matter how many multiplication and divisions are made. His result is yours multiplied by the 'thought' number. When he divides by the thought number his result is exactly yours! Finally when he tells the final result just subtract your result and that is the curious 'thought' number of your friend.

19. Suppose your friend thinks 'x'. You have asked him to multiply by 'a', add 'b' and then divide by 'c' in this sequential order. If you follow the steps given in the problem finally you will get b/c. You are carefully tangling the thread and untangling it!

20. Let us see how this works. Let the sealed number is 32 and the thought number is 75 Following your instructions your friend first gets (75 + 99 – 32) which is 142, a number from 100 to 198. Crossing out first digit and adding to 142 gives 43. Then subtract this 43 from thought number that results as the sealed number!

21.   40 cm.

22.   As for socks are concerned three are ok because definitely two of them will be of same colour. But, in case of gloves minimum I have to take 21. Suppose I take 20 gloves there is a chance of all of them for suitable to left hand only with ten brown and ten black colour.

23. Over time allowance = £500 and basic salary = £4,500

24. Twenty minutes

25. Let the ages be a and b. Then (a x b) + (a + b) + 1 = (a + 1) (b + 1). Hence factorise the result she says and take away 1 from each of them.

26. Let the numbers be a, b, c, and d. According to the instructions you may get [{(2a + 5) 5 + 10 + b}10 + c]10 + d = 200a + 100b + 10c + d + 3500. From the final result 7482 take away 3500 and you get the numbers that he thought i.e. 3, 9, 8 and 2.

27.The reasons behind these peculiar products are 3 x 37 = 111, 7 x 11 x 13 = 1,001 and 3 x 7 x 11 x 13 x 37 = 111,111.

28 Six years.

29. Twenty ducklings. Every time half of them went away and ten of them returned back!

30. Don't do this trick for the second time to the same person. Because always it is elephant!

31. .Her present age is 18.

32. .If somebody answers 5 tea cups you can retard them by saying, "I told sixty cups and one is broken; then will it not be remaining 59?" If somebody says 59, you simply turn the plate! "I told six tea cups; one is broken and how come it will 59 balance?"

33. It is 20%.

34. In case of a) the answer is 25%; but for b) it is not 25% It is $\left[\dfrac{100}{75}-1\right]100=33\%$. Hence instead of increasing the salary the government should see that the prices are reduced. Increase in salary simply lowers the money value.

35. If you say it is 18% then you are wrong! The correct answer is 20%.

36. For one part now he takes 75% of time otherwise in unit time he now does 1.33 amount of work. The increase is 0.33 or 33%.

37. It is not 78.7. The correct answer is 75.9

Sir Isaac Newton (1642 – 1727). He was born in Woolsthrope, Linconshire, England. One of the greatest intellects of all time. He went to Trinity College, Cambridge in 1661 and by the age of 23 he made three discoveries: the nature of colours, the calculus and the law of gravitation. Using calculus he gave explanation of the movement of sun, moon and the stars

10

Number Patterns

Neglect of mathematics works injuries to all knowledge, since he who is ignorant of it cannot know the other sciences or things of this world.

Roger Bacon

Digits can form combination that call to mind the intricate design patterns that we can see around nature.

1.   **Multiplication patterns with remarkable results.**

44
×44
16
+1616
+16
1936

answer

44
× 44
4
+484
484 × 4
1936

888
× 888
64
+ 6464
+ 646464
+ 6464
+ 64
788544

answer

888
× 888
8
+ 888
+ 8888
98568 × 8
788544

137

2.   Diamond shaped Multiplication pattern

888888888888
× 888888888888
64
6464
646464
64646464
6464646464
646464646464
64646464646464
6464646464646464
646464646464646464
64646464646464646464
6464646464646464646464
646464646464646464646464
6464646464646464646464
64646464646464646464
646464646464646464
6464646464646464
64646464646464
646464646464
6464646464
64646464
646464
6464
64
790123456788543209876544

This type of pattern works out successfully for any digits of repeated numbers multiplied by the same. Readers can try for themselves. The above given multiplication is done by another method to get a different pattern in the next page.

3. Pyramid type multiplication pattern

888888888888
× 888888888888
8
888
88888
8888888
888888888
88888888888
8888888888888
888888888888888
88888888888888888
8888888888888888888
888888888888888888888
88888888888888888888888
9876543209856790123456 8 × 8
79012345678854320987654 4

4. 1 to 9 appears only once.

In the following patterns you can see that each digit from 1 to 9 appears once and only once in each of the equations.

1,738 x 4 – 6,952	483 x 12 = 5,796
1,963 x 4 = 7,852	297 x 18 = 5,346
198 x 27 = 5,346	157 x 28 = 4,396
138 x 42 = 5,796	186 x 39 = 7,254

5. Same numbers appear on both sides.

The following equations have the same numbers on both sides even though the operation symbols are different.

$42 \div 3 = 4 \times 3 + 2$;	$\sqrt{121} = 12 - 1$
$63 \div 3 = 6 \times 3 + 3$	$\sqrt{64} = 6 + \sqrt{4}$
$95 \div 5 = 9 + 5 + 5$	$\sqrt{9} + 4 = 9 - \sqrt{4}$
$(2 + 7) \times 2 \times 16 = 272 + 16$;	$\sqrt{169} = 16 - \sqrt{9} = \sqrt{16} + 9$
$5^{6-2} = 625$;	$\sqrt{256} = 2 \times 5 + 6$
$(8 + 9)^2 = 289$;	$\sqrt{324} = 3 \times (2 + 4)$
$2^{10} - 2 = 1,022$;	$\sqrt{11,881} = 118 - 8 - 1$
$2^{8-1} = 128$;	$\sqrt{1,936} = 36 + 9 - 1$

$2^3 \times 4 = 4^3 \div 2 = 34 - 2;$ $\sqrt[3]{1{,}331} = 3 + 3 + 3 + 1 + 1$

6.   Crystal growth in numbers with 16

$$16 = 4^2$$
$$1{,}156 = 34^2$$
$$11{,}156 = 334^2$$
$$11{,}115{,}556 = 3{,}334^2$$
$$1{,}111{,}155{,}556 = 33{,}334^2$$

$111{,}111{,}555{,}556 = 333{,}334^2$, how does this pattern work? If we consider $16 = 10x + y$, no matter how many times we insert in between $(10x + y - 1)$, the new number is a perfect square.

7. Crystal growth with 49

49 is another number which gives growth according to the formula stated in 6.

8. Growth with 9

Here is another type of growth pattern with the number 9. Write it as 09, keep adding 1 on the left and 8 in the second position on the right i.e. add digit one more than 0 and one less than 9.

$$09 = 3^2$$
$$1{,}089 = 33^2$$
$$110{,}889 = 333^2$$
$$11{,}108{,}889 = 3{,}333^2 \text{ etc.}$$

9. Growth with 36

Similarly you can try with 36. The digits added are one more than 3 and one less than 6 as stated in 8.

10.   Can you write 10 using five 9$_s$?

$$9 + \frac{99}{99} = 10,$$ $$\frac{99}{9} - \frac{9}{9} = 10$$

$$\left(9 + \frac{9}{9}\right)^{\frac{9}{9}} = 10$$ $$9 + 99^{9-9} = 10$$

11. **Can you write 100 using all the digits from 0 to 9?**

$$70 + 24\frac{9}{18} + 5\frac{3}{6} = 100,$$ $$80\frac{27}{54} + 19\frac{3}{6} = 100$$

$$87 + 9\frac{4}{5} + 3\frac{12}{60} = 100$$ $$50\frac{1}{2} + 49\frac{38}{76} = 100$$

12. **Different methods of writing 100 using same five digits in each method.**

$$111 - 11 = 100,$$ $$(33x3) + \frac{3}{3} = 100,$$

$$5 \times 5 \times 5 - 5 \times 5 = 100,$$ $$(5 + 5 + 5 + 5) \times 5 = 100.$$

13. **Same numbers on both sides with same results.**
     In the following set of equations a number is multiplied by the sum of its two parts giving the sum of cubes of two parts.

$$37 \times (3 + 7) = 3^3 + 7^3 = 370$$
$$48 \times (4 + 8) = 4^3 + 8^3 = 576$$
$$111 \times (11 + 1) = 11^3 + 1^3 = 1332$$
$$147 \times (14 + 7) = 14^3 + 7^3 = 3087$$
$$148 \times (14 + 8) = 14^3 + 8^3 = 3256$$

14. **Write the numbers 1 to 10 using just five twos.**

$$1 = 2 + 2 - 2 - \frac{2}{2}$$ $$2 = 2 + 2 + 2 - 2 - 2$$

$$3 = 2 + 2 - 2 + \frac{2}{2}$$ $$4 = 2 \times 2 \times 2 - 2 - 2$$

$$5 = 2 + 2 + 2 - \frac{2}{2}$$ $$6 = 2 + 2 + 2 + 2 - 2$$

$$7 = \frac{22}{2} - 2 - 2$$ $$8 = 2 \times 2 \times 2 + 2 - 2$$

$$9 = 2 \times 2 \times 2 + \frac{2}{2}$$ $$10 = 2 + 2 + 2 + 2 + 2$$

15. Numbers 11 to 26, using just five twos only.

Here is something for you to try. Write numbers 11 to 26, using just five twos only. You can use exponents and parenthesis.

16. Numbers 2 to 9 can be expressed by fractions in which every digit except '0' appears once only.

For example:

$$7 = \frac{16,758}{2,394}; \quad 8 = \frac{25,496}{3,187}; \quad 9 = \frac{57,429}{6,381}$$

Similarly try for numbers 2,3,4,.5 and 6.

17. Products can be the reverse of additions. Example:

9 + 9 = 18 but 9 X 9 = 81 which is reverse of 18.

24 + 3 = 27 but 24 X 3 = 72

47 + 2 = 49 but 47 X 2 = 94

497 + 2 = 499, but 497 X 2 = 994

18. Pairs of certain two digit numbers have the same product even when both numbers are reversed. Example:

14 X 82 = 28 X 41 = 1148; 13 X 93 = 39 X 31 = 1209

42 X 12 = 24 X 21 = 504; 12 X 63 = 36 X 21 = 756

12 X 84 = 48 X 21 = 1008; 13 X 62 = 26 X 31 = 806

24 X 84 = 42 X 48 = 2016; 26 X 93 = 39 X 62 = 2418

23 X 96 = 69 X 32 = 2208; 24 X 63 = 36 X 42 = 1512

36 X 84 = 48 X 63 = 3024; 46 X 96 = 69 X 64 = 4416

Can you find two more pairs like this?

19. Squares of certain consecutive numbers have the answers with same digits but in different order.

See examples given below.

$13^2 = 169$ and $14^2 = 196$

$157^2 = 24,649$ and $158^2 = 24,964$

$913^2 = 833,569$ and $914^2 = 835,396$.

20. Can you find the integer of given specifications?

It is a six digits with two odds and four even numbers. It starts with 2, ends with 6 and a 2 in hundreds place? This six-digit integer should have the following properties simultaneously.

a) It is the fourth power of sum of its digits

b) If we separate it into three groups of two digits each, the sum of the two-digit numbers is a square.

c) Even after reversing it satisfies the condition stated in (b)

21. A funny multiplication.

A funny multiplication: 48 X 159 = 7,632. In this equation all digits are different and none is repeated. More examples of similar type are given below.

12 X 483 = 5,790   4 X 1,963 = 7,852

42 X 138 = 5,796   4 x 1,738 = 6,952

18 X 297 = 5,346   28 X 157 = 4,396

27 X 198 = 5,346;   48 X 159 = 7,632

39 X 186 = 7,254

22..   Repeating three digits to get 24.

By writing three eights like this 8 + 8 + 8 we can show the answer is 24. Can you get 24 like this with different digits?

23. Number patterns of 30.

By writing three fives like this, 5 X 5 + 5, we can show the answer is 30. Can you get 30 like this with different digits?

24.   Can you show 1000 as obtained by using same digits of eight numbers?

There are many ways to do this. One of such method is shown here.

888 + 88+ 8 + 8 + 8 = 1000.

25. Constellation of numbers

A constellation of six numbers 2, 3, 7, 1, 5, 6 has the following interesting properties

$2 + 3 + 7 = 1 + 5 + 6 = 12$

$2^2 + 3^2 + 7^2 = 1^2 + 5^2 + 6^2 = 62$

Similar constellations with different numbers are shown below. (Leonard Euler – Swiss Mathematician)

$0 + 5 + 5 + 10 = 1 + 2 + 8 + 9 = 20$

$0^2 + 5^2 + 5^2 + 10^2 = 1^2 + 2^2 + 8^2 + 9^2 = 150$

$0^3 + 5^3 + 5^3 + 10^3 = 1^3 + 2^3 + 8^3 + 9^3 = 1250$

$$1 + 4 + 12 + 13 + 20 = 2 + 3 + 10 + 16 + 19 = 50$$
$$1^2 + 4^2 + 12^2 + 13^2 + 20^2 = 2^2 + 3^2 + 10^2 + 16^2 + 19^2 = 730$$
$$1^3 + 4^3 + 12^3 + 13^3 + 20^3 = 2^3 + 3^3 + 10^3 + 16^3 + 19^3 = 11990$$

26. Constellation with factorial numbers

a) $145 = 1! + 4! + 5! = 1 + 24 + 120$

b) $40,585 = 4! + 0! + 5! + 8! + 5! = 24 + 1 + 120 + 40320$

27. One written with two digits

What is the smallest integer you can write with two digits. If you say 10 it is wrong. The answer is 1. But how is this?

28. One written by using 0 to 9

Can you write number 1 using all the 10 digits from 0 to 9 without repeating the same digit?

29. Balance the equation

I have given below numbers from 9 to 1 in descending order with necessary signs being missed out between them. Can you insert suitable operative signs in place of '£' so that the equation is balanced?

$9 £ 8 £ 7 £ 6 £ 5 £ 4 £ 3 £ 2 £ 1 = 100$

30. Magic with the number 12,345,679

Can you multiply this with any two-digit number having a factor of 9. For example 12,345,679 X 72. You can write the answer immediately as 888,888,888. Similarly the product 12,345,679 X 54 = 666,666,666.

31. Number oddities.

Consider the number $9801 = (98 + 01)^2$. Can you find some more patterns of this type?

32. Numbers primes and composites

Prime numbers have two divisors and composite numbers have three or more divisors. Do not consider repeating divisors. This pattern is followed throughout. Among the divisors one is not a prime number. See the following table

Numbers	Divisors
2	1, 2
3	1, 3
4	1, 2, 4
……..	………
363	3, 11, 363
8648	8, 23, 47, 8648 etc.

33. A palindromic sum

Write any integer of more than one digit and write below its reverse and add. If you don't get the result as palindrome repeat this process again and again.

38	139	48,017
83	931	71,084
---	------	--------
121	1,070	119,101
	701	101,911
	-------	----------
	1,7 71	221,012
		210,122

		431,134

34. Tell at a glance

1	123456789
21	12345678
321	1234567
4321	123456
54321	12345
654321	1234
7654321	123
87654321	12
987654321	1

The above two column of numbers are similar but up side down. If you sum up this which one will give larger total?

Answers: Number patterns

7. $49 = 7^2$
    $4,489 = 67^2$
    $444,889 = 667^2$
    $44,448,889 = 6,667^2$

9. $36 = 6^2$
    $4,356 = 66^2$
    $443,556 = 666^2$

15.
$11 = 22 \div 2 + 2 - 2;$	$12 = 2 \times 2 \times 2 + 2 + 2$
$13 = (22 + 2 + 2) \div 2$	$14 = 2 \times 2 \times 2 \times 2 - 2$
$15 = 22 \div 2 + 2 + 2;$	$16 = (2 \times 2 + 2 + 2) \times 2$
$17 = (2 \times 2)^2 + 2/2;$	$18 = 2 \times 2 \times 2 \times 2 + 2$
$19 = 22 - 2 - 2/2;$	$20 = 22 + 2 - 2 - 2;$
$21 = 22 - 2 + 2/2;$	$22 = 22 \times 2 - 22$
$23 = 22 + 2 - 2/2;$	$24 = 22 - 2 + 2 + 2;$
$25 = 22 + 2 + 2/2;$	$26 = 2 \times (22 / 2 + 2)$

16. $\dfrac{13,458}{6,729} = 2; \quad \dfrac{17,485}{2,697} = 3; \quad \dfrac{15,768}{3,942} = 4$

$\dfrac{13,485}{2697} = 5; \quad \dfrac{17,658}{2,943} = 6; \quad \dfrac{97,524}{10,836} = 9 =$

$\dfrac{97,524}{10,836} = \dfrac{57,429}{06,381} = \dfrac{95,823}{10,647} = \dfrac{95,742}{10,638} = \dfrac{75,249}{08,361} = \dfrac{58,239}{06,471}$

18. $34 \times 86 = 43 \times 68; 23 \times 64 = 32 \times 46$

20. 234256. $22^4 = 234256$; $23 + 42 + 56 = 121$ also $65 + 24 + 32 = 121$ which is a square number.

22. $22 + 2; 3^3 - 3$

23. $6 \times 6 - 6; 3^3 + 3; 33 - 3.$

147

27. Number 1 can be written in infinite ways like 1/1; 2/2; 3/3........etc. Also 54^0, 67^0; 458^0 ....etc. any number divided by the same number or any number raised to the power of zero.

28. $\dfrac{148}{296} + \dfrac{35}{70} = 1$; $(123456789)^0$ and $(234567)^{9-8-1}$

29. There are three possible ways to do this.
    $(9 \times 8) + 7 + 6 + 5 + 4 + (3 \times 2 \times 1) = 100$
    $\{(1+2+3+4+5) \times 6\} - 7 + 8 + 9 = 100$
    $1 - 2 + (3 \times 4 \times 5) + (6 \times 7) + 8 - 9 = 100$

30. $12{,}345{,}679 \times 9 = 111{,}111{,}111$

31. $3025 = (30 + 25)^2$, $2025 = (20 + 25)^2$. To my knowledge I couldn't find any more of this pattern.

34. They have equal total.

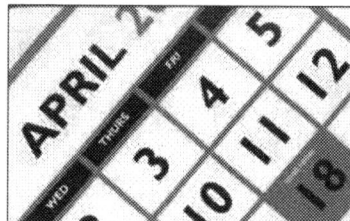

11

Everlasting Calendar

1.   Tell me your date of birth I will tell you the day.

If anybody says the date, month and year of any event, say birth, graduation etc. you can, after a little bit of working announce the day of the week of that particular event. Of course little bit of remembrance and practice is needed. Each month has been assigned with Significant Value (SV), which varies for each century. The following table 1 gives this SV.

Table 1

century		Jan	Feb	Mar	Apl	May	Jun
17th	Jan.1,1600 to Dec.31, 1699	3	6	6	2	4	0
18th	Jan.1, 1700 to Dec.31,1799	2	5	5	1	3	6
19th	Jan.1, 1800 to Dec.31, 1899	1	4	4	0	2	5
20th	Jan.1, 1900 to Dec.31, 1999	0	3	3	6	1	4
21st	Jan.1, 2000 to Dec.31, 2099	6	2	2	5	0	3
22nd	Jan.1, 2100 to Dec.31, 2199	5	1	1	4	6	2
23rd	Jan.1, 2200 to Dec.31, 2299	4	0	0	3	5	1

century		July	Aug	Sep	Oct	Nov	Dec
17th	Jan.1,1600 to Dec.31, 1699	2	5	1	3	6	1
18th	Jan.1, 1700 to Dec.31,1799	1	4	0	2	5	0
19th	Jan.1, 1800 to Dec.31, 1899	0	3	6	1	4	6
20th	Jan.1, 1900 to Dec.31, 1999	6	2	5	0	3	5
21st	Jan.1, 2000 to Dec.31, 2099	5	1	4	6	2	4
22nd	Jan.1, 2100 to Dec.31, 2199	4	0	3	5	1	3
23rd	Jan.1, 2200 to Dec.31, 2299	3	6	2	4	0	2

We know that a leap year is divisible by 4 without a remainder. For example 2000 was a leap year and 2004 also be a leap year. When you are working with a leap year, deduct 1 from SV given in Table 1 only for months January or February.
In addition, each day of the week is assigned with a number as shown Table 2.

Table 2

Sunday	0
Monday	1
Tuesday	2
Wednesday	3
Thursday	4
Friday	5
Saturday	6

Let us consider 18th November 1997. What day it was?
Take the last two digits of the year i.e.97 and divide it by 4. Consider only the quotient, in this case it is 24 and omit the remainder.

Add it back to the year, 97 + 24 = 121

To this add the date, 121 + 18 = 139

From Table 1 the SV for November 1997, 20th century is 3. Add this to 139 which comes to 142.

Divide this 142 by 7 and consider <u>only the remainder</u> which is 2
From Table 2, the day for 2 is Tuesday.

<u>Hence November 18, 1997 is Tuesday</u>

The method shown in the previous page can be expressed in a formula,
Day of the week = The remainder of

$$\frac{\left[\dfrac{quotient\ of\ (year)}{4} \right] + year + day + SV}{7}$$

Mrs. Linnet got a baby born on January 1st , 2000. What day it was? SV is the value taken from Table 1 less 1 since 2000 is a leap year i.e. $6 - 1 = 5$.
Using the formula

$$\frac{\dfrac{00}{4} + 00 + 1 + 5}{7} = 0R6$$

from Table 2 we get 6 represents **Saturday.**

2.   Certain Facts on our calendar:

The Gregorian calendar came into use in 1582. The Babylonians , who developed a sophisticated knowledge of astronomy and mathematics, made closer observations and figured a year was about 360 days. They divided a year into 10 periods of 36 days each. Of course this do not agree with the lunar phases. By Roman times, several of the months had been taken on names of their customs.

January, from *Janus*, the two-faced God who looks forward and backward.
February named after a Roman festival, *Februa*.
March after *Mars*, the Roman God of war. The first month for Romans.
April from Latin, the month of Venus
May from *Maia*, the Goddess of increase.
June, from the name of famous roman family, *Junius*.
July, the month of *Julius Caesar*.
August, the month of *Augustus Caesar*.

September, the Romans' seventh month.
October, the eighth month
November, the ninth month
December, the tenth month

3. Shall I find your age?

Ask your friend to write the number of his birth month. Let him do the following steps to the out coming results of each process. Multiply his birth month by 2; add 5; multiply by 50 and add 1455. From this total let him subtract year of his birth. Ask your friend to tell the resulting number. The last two digits of the final number is his present age.

Example: If he had born on June 1974 then it works as follows. 6 x 2 = 12; 12 + 5 = 17; 17 x 50 = 850;
850 + 1455 = 2305; 2305 – 1974 = 331. The last two digits i.e. numbers in the unit and tenth place are 3 and 1 and the age is 31!
Here is one more example. I am born in January of 1938.
1 x 2 =2; 2 + 5 = 7; 7 x 50 = 350; 350 + 1455 = 1805. In this case 1805 is smaller than my year of birth i.e. 1938. Hence take 1805 as 2805 by adding 1000 and then subtract 1938. 2805 – 1938 = 867 and my age is 67 completed.
Note: The number added in the 4th step, 1455 is for this current year 2005. Add 1 to 1455 for every successive year after 2005.

4. Double guessing.

A simple mathematical working can enable to tell any number your friend thinks of and also his age. Ask your friend to select any number of any size. Let him double it, add 5 and multiply the result by 50. Now ask him to add 1755 to the result followed by subtracting his year of birth. Ask him to tell the final result. The last two figure is his age and the other remaing number is his thought number. See the following example. Mrs. Rita is born on June 1974 and she thinks 21.

21 x 2 = 42; 42 + 5 = 47; 47 x 50 = 2350; 2350 + 1755 = 4105; 4105 – 1974 = 2131. Her age is 31 and she thought of the number 21. Note that the addition of 1755 is valid for only this year i.e.2005. Add 1 to 1755 for every successive year after 2005.

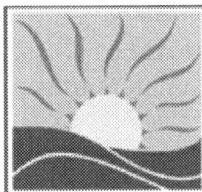

12

QUICK MATHS

1. Squaring a two digit number ending with 5

Suppose we want to find 65^2, Number 5 is in the unit place and square it, which gives 25. In the 10th place we have 6 and multiply it with its next number i.e. 7
$6 \times 7 = 42$
Therefore, $65^2 = 4225$.
Try to find the values of 85^2, 105^2 and check with your calculator.

2. Squaring a two digit number beginning with 5

Suppose we want to find 59^2. The number in the 10th place is 5. Square it and add to the number in the unit place i.e. $5^2 + 9 = 25 + 9 = 34$. The square value of the number in the unit place is $9^2 = 81$. Therefore $59^2 = 3481$.
Try yourself similar games and check with calculator.

3. Product of two digit numbers

Suppose you want to find 76 x 34 quickly without calculator.
Here is a method!

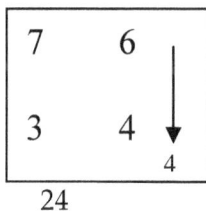

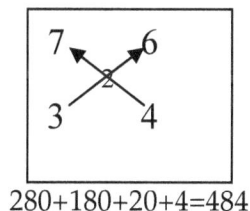

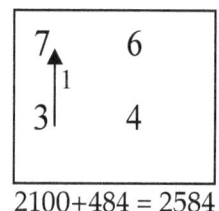

7 6 ↓	7 ✕ 6	7 6
3 4 ↓4	3 4	3 4
24	280+180+20+4=484	2100+484 = 2584

: 6 x 4 = 24. Write 4 and carry over 2 with the product sum of 3 x 6 and 4 x 7 which is 18 + 28 + 2 = 48. Write 8 next to 4 as 84. 7 times 3 is 21 and plus the carryover 4 makes 25. Therefore the product is 2584.

Practice is better than reading. Try as many as possible and check with calculator.

4. Multiplication with 11
There are two ways to play this game.

Method 1: Suppose you want multiply 35 X 11. Write the sum of the two digits of 35 i.e. 3 + 5 = 8. Write 8 to the right side and 3 to the left side of 8. i.e. in between 3 and 5. There you get the result 35 X 11 = 385. How simple it is! Maths is a so lovely a game to enjoy and play!

Suppose you have to do 69 X 11. As before 9 + 6 = 15. Insert 5 in the middle and carry over 1 to left side and add with 6 to get 7 the rest is as before. So the answer you get will be 759.

Method 2: Suppose you want to multiply 427 X 11.
First do 427 X 10 = 4270 and add 427.

```
427 X 10 =     4270
              +427
              ----
               4697
```

5. Multiplication with two digits numbers ending with 1 like 21, 31, 41, ...91.
Suppose you want to do 52 X 81. First multiply 52 with 8 and put a zero to the right end. Then to this add 52 and get the answer! Here you see
52 X 8 = 416 and put 0 before 8 = 4160 and add 52. Hence you get the final answer 4212.

Try some more games like this.

6. Multiplication of a number with 15
Suppose you want to do 102 X 15. Find half of 102 that is 51. Add this 51 to 102 that comes to 153. Now multiply this 153 with 10 and there you get the answer as 1530

Suppose you have to do 137 X 15. Follow this

Half of 137 is 68.5

```
          137.0
         +68.5
         --------
```

205.5 X 10 = 2055 is the answer

7. Multiplication trick with 45
Suppose you want to multiply   142 X 45.
Mentally do   142 X 50   = 7100
Find one tenth of 7100   = -710
Subtracting, we get the answer   = 6390
Suppose it is 19 X 45
19 x 50 = 950: 950 – 95 = 855 answer

8. Multiplication trick with 55
Suppose it is required 64 X 55
Mentally do   64 X 50 = 3200
Find one tenth of 3200   + 320
Adding, we get the answer   = 3520

9. Multiplying by 9
Suppose 13 X 9
Multiply 13 by 10 and subtract 13
13 X 10 – 13 = 130 – 13 = 117 is the answer

10. Multiplying by a number that is a multiple of 9
Suppose we want 57 X 45
The next number to 45 with 0 in unit place is 50.
So find mentally   57 X 50 = 2850
Subtract one tenth of this product   285
The answer is   2565

Try these problems 75 X 15, 56 X 45, 123 X 55 and check your answers with a calculator.

11. Multiplying by a number that is a multiple of 99

Suppose we want to find 297 X 23. Here 297 is a multiple of 99. The next higher
number ending with 0 is 300. Hence find   23 X 300   = 6900
Subtract one hundredth of this product   = - 69
So we get the answer   = 6831

*In the following few cases the author wishes to introduce the principles of Indian Vedic
mathematics. Sthaptyaveda consists of many sutras (formulae) concerned with
engineering and mathematics.*

12. Multiplying two of two digit numbers slightly less than 100 using Nikhilam Sutra.

Suppose we want to do 93 X 94. Take base number as 100. Write 93 and 94 one below the other. To the right side write the corresponding differences from the base 100 as shown in the box. Write the product of the difference column on the right side of stroke. Write the difference of any one diagonal on the left side of the stroke. Then you get the answer. Follow the steps shown in the box.
7 X 6 = 42 and 93 – 6 or 94 – 7 = 87. Hence the answer is 8742.

```
93       7  (100 – 93)

94       6  (100 – 94)

87   /   42 = 8742

Answer is 8742
```

Let us try one more example on this Nikhilam Sutra method
Suppose you want to multiply 97 X 88. Let us try same procedures. Here also the base is 100

```
85       15

88       12

73 1 /  180  Take 1 as
             carry over to
             the right side
             of stroke
Answer is 7480
```

13. Multiplying two of three digit numbers slightly less than 1000 using Nikhilam Sutra.

Suppose we have to do 988 X 887. Following same procedures:

998	12
992	8
980 / 96	But one can guess the answer should have 6 digits. Hence write the answer as **980096**

14. To find the square of 999986

Take 1000000 as the working base and following the same procedure

999986	14	
999986	14	(answer must be 12 digits)
999972	196	

Hence $999986^2 = 999972000196$

15. To find the product of two numbers one greater than 100 and other less than 100

Suppose we want to find 89 X 112. Now also the base is 100

89	-11
112	+12
101	-132

And the answer is $10100 - 132 = 9968$

16. To find the product of two numbers greater than the working base

Suppose it is required to find 108 X 112

108	+8
112	+12 (Here it should be 108 + 12 or 112 + 8)
120	96 and the answer is 12096

17. To find the product of two numbers with any other bases

Suppose we have to find the value of 488 X492.
Now let us take 500 as the base. Since 500 X 2 = 1000

488	-12
492	-8
480	96

the answer is $(480000 / 2) + 96 = 240096$, here we divide 480000 by 2 because the base is 500 instead of 1000.

Suppose it is 507 X 492. Following the same procedure and 500 is the base

507	+7
492	-8
499	-56

the answer is $(499000 / 2) - 56 = 249444$

18. Squaring a number ending with 5

Already we have seen this case in 2, for two digits numbers. Same method applies for three digits also. Suppose we want to find 965^2. First find 96 X 97 by using Nikilam Sutra method shown in 11.

96	4
97	3
93	12

and hence 96 X 97 = 9,312. and $5^2 = 25$.
Therefore $965^2 = 931,225$.

19. Squaring a number near to 50.

Suppose we want to find 47^2. Let us use the Nikilam Sutra method. 47 is short of 50 by 3. $3^2 = 9$

$47 - 3 = 44$ and half of 44 is 22 and hence $47^2 = 2209$.

We find half of 44 because 50 is the base.

Let us see one more example. Suppose we want to find 57^2. In this case 50 is the base

57	7
57	7
64	49

The answer is $(64 / 2) + 49 = 3249$.

20. Squaring a number ending with 1.

Suppose we want to find the value of 71^2, consider 71 as $70 + 1$. Square of 70 is 4900. Add to this $(70 + 71) = 141$. Therefore $71^2 = 4,900 + 141 = 5,041$. How simple it is!

One more example: Find 141^2. First find $140^2 = 19,600$ and add to this $140 + 141 = 281$. therefore $141^2 = 19,600 + 281 = 19,881$.

21. Squaring a number ending with 9.

Let us see the example 89^2. We know $90^2 = 8,100$ to this subtract $(90 + 89) = 179$, we get 7921. Let us do one more example. 349^2. $350^2 = 122,500$ see prob.2. Hence the answer for $349^2 = 122,500 - 699 = 121,801$.

22. Squaring a number ending with 4.

The method shown in previous case can also be used here. Suppose we want to find 54^2. First find $55^2 = 3,025$ (refer prob.2). From this subtract $(55 + 54 = 109)$. The answer is 2,916.

23. Squaring any number.

Nikilam Sutra method explained in 11 may be useful. Let us find the value of 784^2.

784	216	
784	216	1000 is the base hence 1000 - 216
568	216^2	as a part of this problem let us find 216^2

216   16
216   16   taking 200 as the base, hence 216 + 16 = 232
─────────

232/5 256   this is equal to 46400 + 256 = 46,656.
Hence 784^2 = 568,000 + 46,656 = 614,656.

24. Area of a table cloth.

My study-table is covered by a cloth measuring 2m-78cm in length and 1m-35cm in width. Find its area. Let us find simply the product of 278 X 135 by any quick method. Suppose we want to find the following algebraic product
$(ax^2 + bx + c)(dx^2 + ex + f)$ which becomes
$x^4 (ad) + x^3 (ae + bd) + x^2 (af + cd + be) + x (bf + ce) + cf$. But, how this is done quickly?

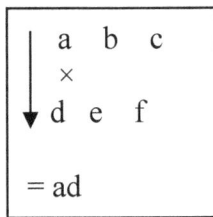

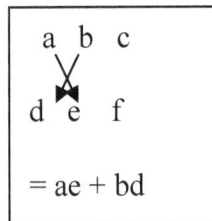

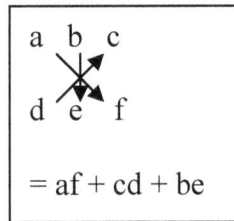

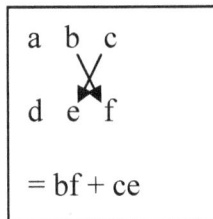

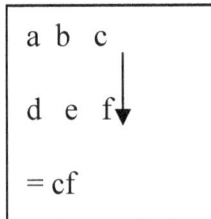

Using the same procedure find the product of 278 X 135 = 37,530. Hence the area of table cloth is 3,753 m².

25. Expressway to find square root.

Find the Square root of 61. The nearest integer that is the square root of 61 is 7. Divide mentally 61 by this nearest integer i.e. 7. We get 8.71. Find the difference between this 8.71 and the nearest square rooting integer i.e. 7. We get 1.71. Half of this difference is 0.855. Always round off this to lower value because the square root obtained by this method is always on the higher side to the actual value given by a calculator. Add this 0.8 to the first approximate and hence $\sqrt{61} = 7.8$. The calculator value is 7.8102.

26. Square root of a bigger number.

Let us find the value of $\sqrt{98,560.872}$. Write the given number in groups of pairs from the last digit, as shown below.

9 85 60. 87 20. The integer first approximate square root is 300 because square root of 9 is 3 and every group of two digits will have one digit in square root. Divide 98,560. 872 by 300. It is easy to do this. First divide by 3 and put the decimal point before the last two digits. We get 328. 53. Take away 300 from this and we get 28.53. Find one half value of this and add to estimate 300 and we get the square root value as 314.2 whereas the calculator value is 313.94 and the percentage of error is +0.083%.

27. Solving quadratic equation easily.

We know that the quadratic equation $ax^2 + bx + c = 0$ has roots given by

$$\frac{-b \pm \sqrt{b^2 - 4ac}}{2a}$$

. Many students find this equation too difficult to remember and get confused in its application. Here is a simple way to solve quadratic equations. Differentiate the expression $ax^2 + bx + c$ which we get as $2ax + b$ and equate this to

the discrimnant of the quadratic expression, $\pm\sqrt{b^2 - 4ac}$

Therefore, $2ax + b = \pm\sqrt{b^2 - 4ac}$ and solve for x.

Let us workout a simple example.
Solve $7x^2 - 25x + 9 = 0$. Differentiate and equate to the discrimnant.
$14x - 25 = \pm 19.31$ which gives $x = 3.165$ or 0.41
Check your answers by summing and multiplying the roots and compare with –
sum of roots = $-b/a$ and product of roots = c/a.

28. Reciprocal quadratic equation.

Suppose we have to solve the following equation

$$\frac{x+4}{x-4} + \frac{x-4}{x+4} = \frac{10}{3}$$

, the usual procedure is to cross multiply and get the quadratic equation as $x^2 = 64$ and $x = \pm 8$. But the quick way to get the result is to write the problem as

$$\frac{x+4}{x-4} + \frac{x-4}{x+4} = \frac{10}{3} = 3 + 1/3.$$

$$\frac{x+4}{x-4} = 3 \text{ and } x = 8$$

also

$$\frac{x+4}{x-4} = \frac{1}{3} \text{ and } x = -8$$

. The above method is known as 'Vilokanam sub-sutra' in Hindu Vedic Mathematics.

29. One more of above type.

Quickly solve the following. This method in Vedhic Maths is known as 'Sunyam samuccaya sutra'.

$$\frac{2x+11}{2x-11} + \frac{2x-11}{2x+11} = \frac{193}{84}$$. The right side value 193/84 can be written in reciprocal

format like $\frac{12}{7} + \frac{7}{12}$. Hence we can equate $\frac{2x+11}{2x-11} = \frac{12}{7}$ or $\frac{7}{12}$. Therefore we get $x = \pm 20.9$.

30. Special type of quadratic equation.

This method in Vedic Maths is known as Sunyam Anyat sutra.

$$\frac{7x+5}{9x-5} = \frac{9x+7}{7x+17}$$ In such an equation the speciality is the sum of the numerators is equal to sum of the denominators i.e $7x + 5 + 9x + 7 = 9x - 5 + 7x + 17 = 16x + 12$. Equate this to zero. Hence $16x + 12 = 0$ and one value of $x = -0.75$. The difference between the numerator and denominator is $7x + 5 - 9x + 5 = -2x + 10$ equate this to 0 and we get the other root $x = 5$.

31. Another special type.

This method is known as Samaya samuccaya sutra.

$$\frac{2}{x+2} + \frac{3}{x+3} = \frac{4}{x+4} + \frac{1}{x+1}$$, In this type of problem you can notice that the sum of the numerator and sum of the denominators on both side of the equation are the same. Take any one side and add the denominators i.e. $2x + 5$ and equate to zero, $2x + 5 = 0$ and $x = -2.5$. The other value of $x = 0$.

32. Equation of a straight line

Suppose we want to find the equation of the straight line joining two points (15, 16) and (9, - 3). Try this with your usual irksome and long method. The Hindu Vedic method gives a simple way for this! Suppose the points are (a, b) and (c, d). The coefficient of x is $(b - d)$ and coefficient of y is $- (a - c)$. The constant at the right hand side is given by $(bc - ad)$. Therefore the equation of the line is

$x(b - d) - y(a - c) = (bc - ad)$.
If the points are (15, 16) and (9, - 3) then the equation of line joining them is
$x(16 - - 3) - y(15 - 9) = (144 - - 45)$
$19x - 6y = 189$. So simple!
 Find the equation of line joining (9, 17) and (7, - 2). The answer will be $19x - 2y =$
137.

33. Cubes & cube roots of simple numbers.
Cubes of first nine natural numbers are 1, 8, 27, 64, 125, 216, 343, 512 and 729.
Remembering this will help us to solve problems involving with cube roots.
Therefore, the last digit of an exact cube is obvious.

If the cube ends in 1, the cube root ends in 1
If the cube ends in 2, the cube root ends in 8
If the cube ends in 3, the cube root ends in 7
If the cube ends in 4, the cube root ends in 4
If the cube ends in 5, the cube root ends in 5
If the cube ends in 6, the cube root ends in 6
If the cube ends in 7, the cube root ends in 3
If the cube ends in 8, the cube root ends in 2
If the cube ends in 9, the cube root ends in 9
If the cube ends in 0, the cube root end in 0

34. Quick cube roots.
To find the cube root of 224. From 32 above the first estimate is 6 because 224 is in
between 216 and 343. Find $224 \div 6 = 37.33$.
Divide 37.33 by 6 again. $37.33 \div 6 = 6.22$
From 6.22 take away the first estimate, 6 i.e. 0.22.
Divide 0.22 by 3, we get 0.07.
 The approximate cube root of 224 is 6.07 where as exact value is 6.0732.

This method gives answer on the higher side. Hence round off always to the
lower values.

35. Second example of cube root:
To find the cube root of 710. This number 710 is very close to 729 compared with
512. Therefore take the first estimate as 9.
$710 \div 9 = 78.88$ (rounded off to lower digit) $78.88 \div 9 = 8.76$. The first digit of the
cube root is 8.
Subtract this 8 from 8.76. We get 0.76

Add 2 to 0.76, we get 2.76.

Divide by 3, 2.76 ÷ 3 = 0.92.

Therefore the cube root of 710 = 8.92. The exact value is also the same!

36. Third example of cube root:

To find the cube root of 7,609.

The first digit 7 is close to 8 and since the given number is of 4 digits the first estimate can be taken as 20.

7609 ÷ 20 = 380.45;

380.45 ÷ 20 = 19.0225. Hence the tens digit of the cube root is 1.

Take away 10. i.e. 19.0225 − 10 = 9.0225

Add 20 + 9.0225 = 29 .0225.

Divide this by 3, we get 9.674.

Therefore the cube root of 7609 = 10 + 9.674 = 19.674. The exact value is also the same!

13. TRICKS WITH MATCH STICKS

Match sticks, tooth pricks or straw tubes used for drinks are ideal for these games. The condition is that they must of same length not bent or broken. These are ideal geometrical amusement games to sharpen the mind of children.

1. **Making squares with 24 sticks**

    How many identical squares can you make with 24 sticks? You should not break them!

    a) Two identical squares each having 3 sticks for one of their sides.
    b) Three identical squares each having two sticks for one of their sides.
    c) But actually you can make not two but three overlapping squares with 3 matches on a side. Figure shown below is one of them.

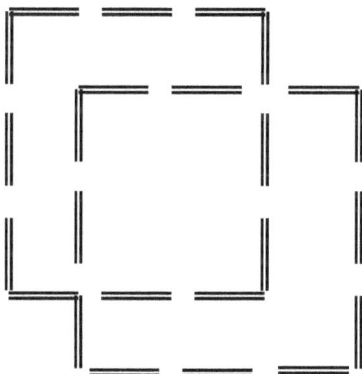

    Try one more
    like this for
    your-self

    d) Try yourselves to get 7 squares in all using two sticks for a side. It will be something like what we have seen in the case of trick (c). Figure is shown below.

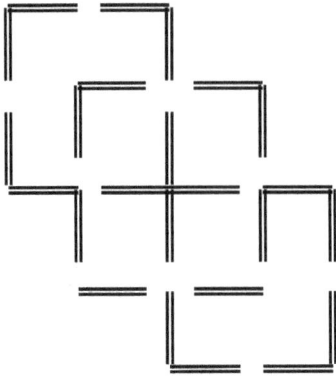

e) Show different cases with one stick on each side. Figures are shown below.

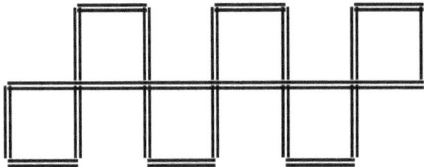

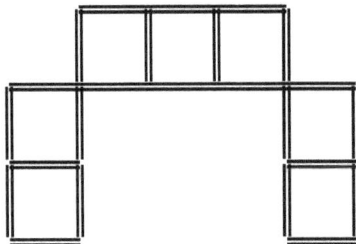

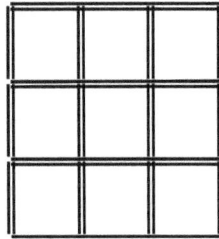

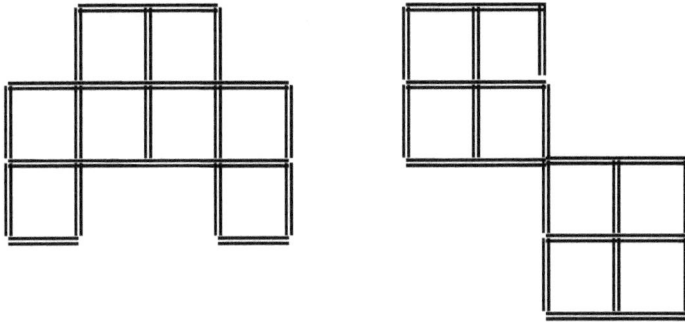

2.   Wine cup and ice cube

The following figure represents a cup made up of four matchsticks and an ice cube out side. It may be easy to pick up the ice cube and drop into the cup containing wine. But can you make the cube go into the cup by just moving not more than two sticks.

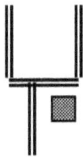

3.   Making squares with 12 sticks.

The following figure shows four unit squares made up of 12 matchsticks.

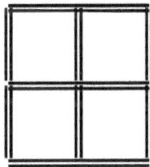

a)   Remove 2 sticks leaving 2 squares of different sizes.

b)   Move three matches to form three identical squares

c)   Move four sticks to form three identical squares.

d)   Move two matches to get seven squares, not all identical. You can cross one stick over other.

e)   Move four matches to form ten different squares, Some sticks may cross.

4. 3 × 3 squares with 24 matchsticks.

The following figure shows 9 unit squares with totally 24 matchsticks.

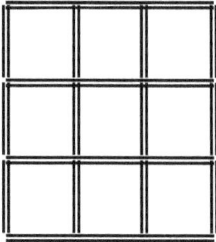

a)   Move 12 matches to make 2 identical squares.
b)   Remove 4 matches leaving one large and 4 small squares.
c)   Form 5 unit squares by removing 4, 6 or 8 sticks.
d)   Remove 8 sticks leaving 4 unit squares.
e)   Remove 6 sticks leaving 3 squares.
f)   Remove 8 sticks leaving 2 squares.
g)   Remove 8 sticks leaving 3 squares.
h)   Remove 6 sticks leaving 2 irregular but identical hexagons and 2 squares.

5. Making squares with 9 sticks

Using 9 matchsticks form 6 squares. Sticks may cross over one another.

6. Church front transforms into squares.

With 13 sticks the following figure of an ancient church entrance is made. Just move 4 sticks and get 11 squares with a triangle. Also move 6 sticks and get 19 squares.

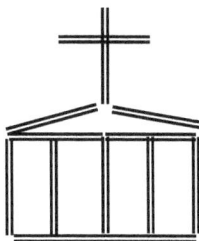

7. **Square by moving one stick**

   Make a square by moving only one strip of the following cross.

   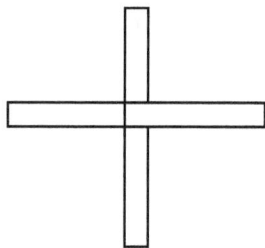

8. **Kilometre problem**

   There are twelve match sticks of each 5 cm long. Put them together to get one kilometre. You are not allowed to add any more or to discard any of the 12 sticks.

9. **Twelve sticks**

   Use the same 12 sticks of the above problem to form
   a) Six equilateral triangles.
   b) A wind mill with three identical wings.

10. **Correct the equation.**

    Wrong equation given below is made up of 23 match sticks. Move only one stick to a different position in the equation to set the sum correct.

    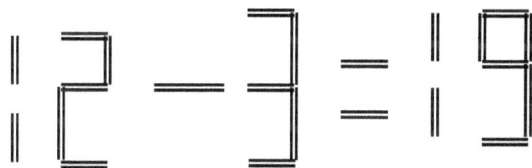

11. **Seven matchsticks to write one third.**

    Arrange seven matchsticks to represent one seventh like shown below. Without adding or removing any sticks just only by moving the existing sticks can you get a fraction that equals to $\dfrac{1}{3}$

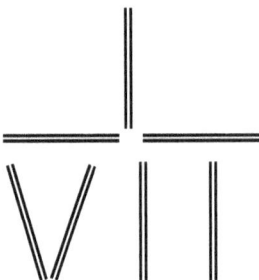

12. Polygons with 8 sticks.

The figures below show that different polygons made with 8 matchsticks. Each of them has different areas.

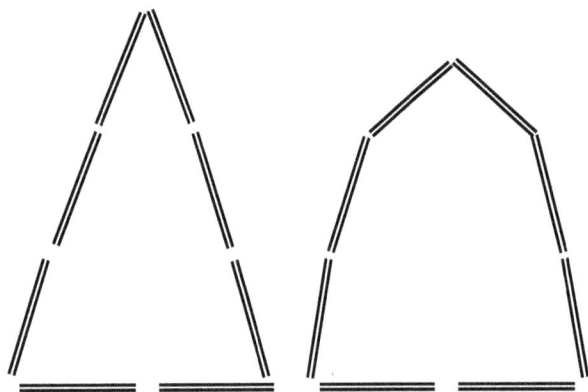

Can you form a polygonal shape with these eight sticks to have the biggest area?

13. A cross with 12 sticks.

The following figure of a cross is made with 12 matches of each measuring 2 cm so that the area of the given figure is 20 cm². Can you rearrange these 12 sticks to get a geometrical shape whose area will be equal to 16 cm²?

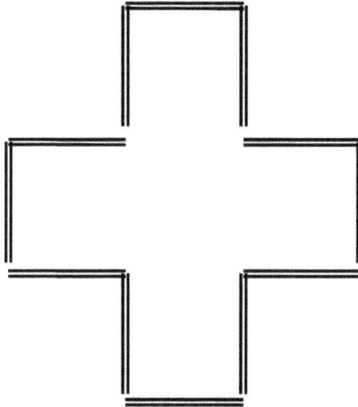

Answers: Tricks with match sticks

1.

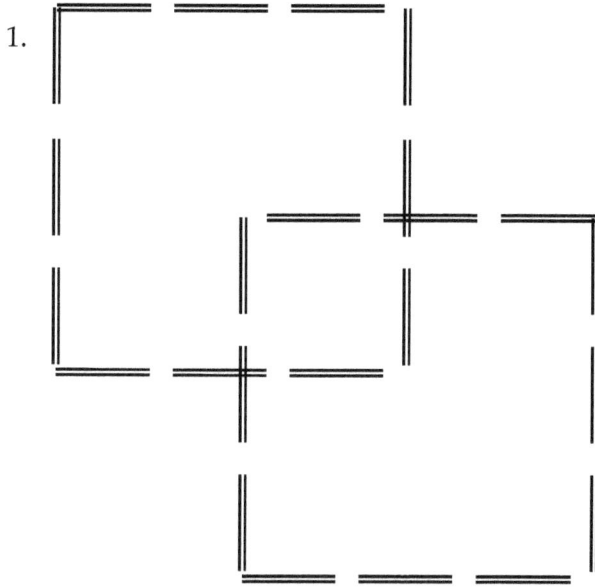

2.

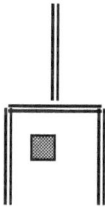

3. a) 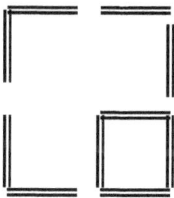 b)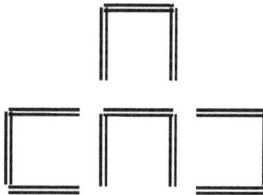

c)

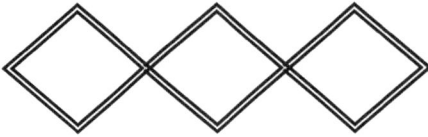

d) 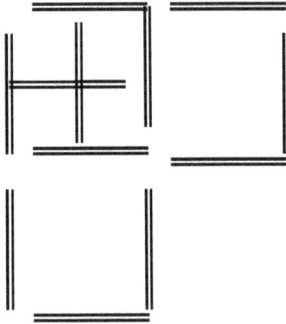   e)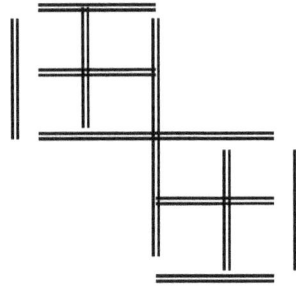

4.

a) Remove all the twelve sticks inside the large square and put them next as an identical large square.

b)

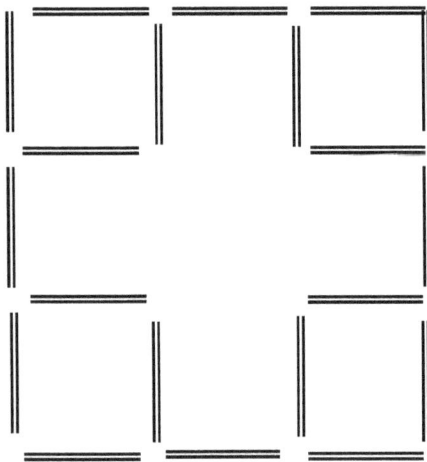

c)

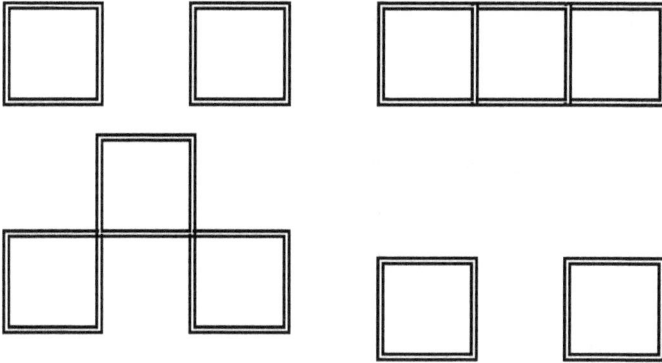

5 squares by removing 4 sticks.   5 squares by removing 6

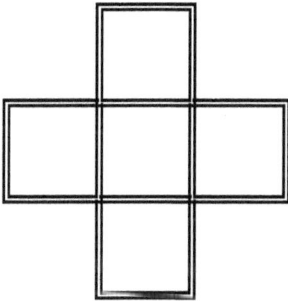

5 squares by removing 8 sticks

d)

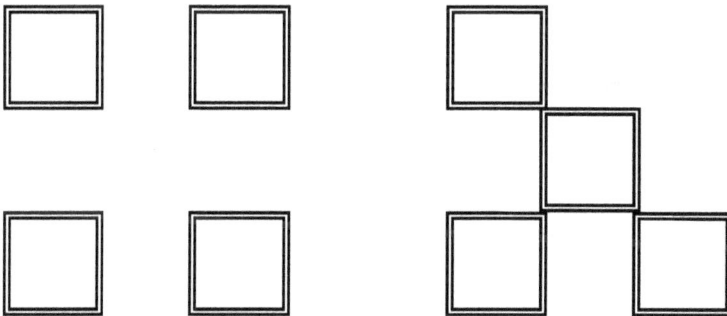

e)

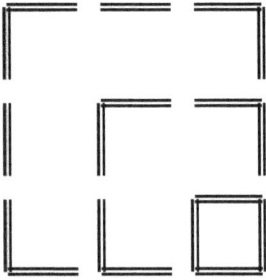

f)

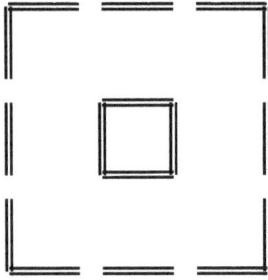

g)

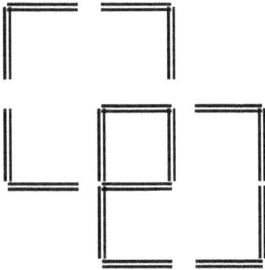

h)

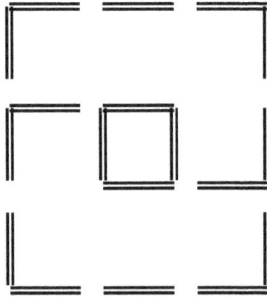

5

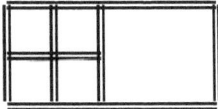

6.

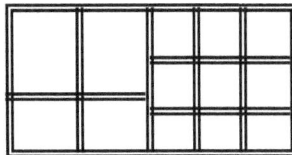

7. Move the right side stripe little farther to the right to form a small square space in the centre. Refer figure shown below.

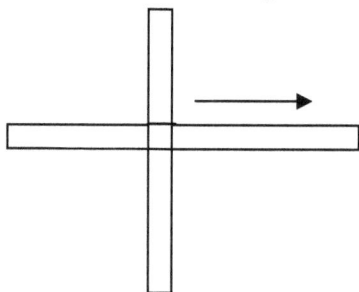

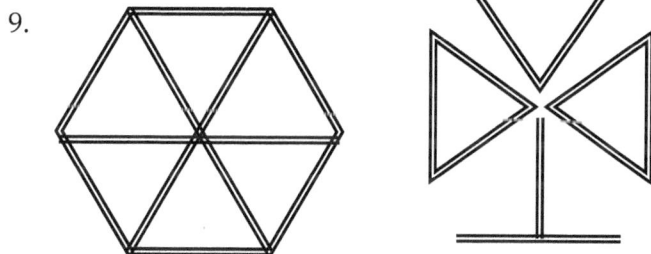

8.

9.

10. Remove one vertical stick from 9 on the right side. Bring to the left side make the minus sign as plus sign. Then it becomes 12 + 3 = 15.

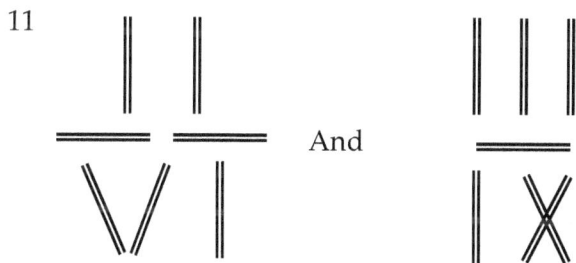

11

And

12. Because we have to use eight match sticks only the octagonal shape is the one enclosing the biggest area.

13.

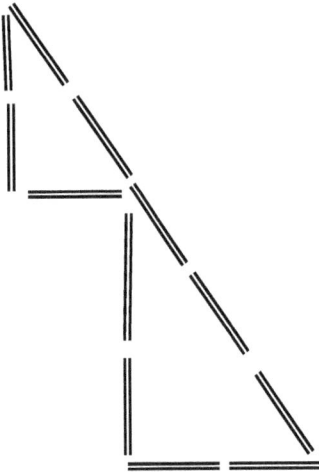

Index

www.ingramcontent.com/pod-product-compliance
Lightning Source LLC
Chambersburg PA
CBHW062042090426
42740CB00016B/2997